CELEBRATING THE MYSTERY OF FAITH

CELEBRATING THE MYSTERY OF FAITH

A Guide to the Mass

NATIONAL CENTRE FOR LITURGY

First published 2005 by
Irish Liturgical Publications
7/8 Lower Abbey Street
Dublin 1
Ireland
Email ilp@veritas.ie

ISBN 0 95498 181 2

A catalogue record for this book is available from the British Library.

Cover: *The Last Supper* by Giovanni Lanfranco
reproduced courtesy of the National Gallery of Ireland
Designed by Colette Dower
Printed in the Republic of Ireland by Paceprint, Dublin

CONTENTS

FOREWORD

This study guide to the celebration of Mass was prepared by a team from the National Centre for Liturgy, including Moira Bergin, Seán Collins, Jane Ferguson, Patrick Jones, Julie Kavanagh, Columba J. McCann, Liam Tracey and Tom Whelan.

Some of the material is based on pastoral notes prepared during the 1990s by ICEL. This material has been updated in the light of the new edition of the *General Instruction of the Roman Missal*. References in footnotes are given throughout this guide to the *General Instruction* so that the reader or study group may have ease of access to the key document.

All references to the *General Instruction* are to the edition for Ireland, published by Irish Liturgical Publications.

After an introductory statement on the Eucharist (Chapter one), and an introduction to *General Instruction* (Chapter two), three chapters put together material which is to be found in different places within the *General Instruction*. Chapter three treats assembly and the ministries that serve our Eucharistic celebration. Chapter four, under the title, The Eucharistic Celebration and its Symbols, is about the cluster of symbols, the actions, objects and words that is our liturgy. Music, though also treated under ministries, is the subject of Chapter five. These chapters serve as background to Chapter six that takes the reader through the Mass. Two chapters of the *General Instruction* consider the choice of texts for the Mass. This is referred to in Chapter seven of this guide, which also summarises the last and new chapter of the *General Instruction* on adaptations.

Finally a parish based study of the *General Instruction*, in five sessions, completes this guide. This liturgical catechesis opens the richness of the *General Instruction* to a parish liturgy team but always with the objective of a celebration of the Mystery of Faith, the Eucharist, that is worthy of God who gifts us with the salvation of Jesus Christ.

DOCUMENTS AND ABBREVIATIONS

DD   *Dies Domini*, Apostolic letter of Pope John Paul II, Keeping the Lord's Day Holy (1998)

EM   *Eucharisticum mysterium*, on the worship of the Eucharist (1967)

EP   *Eucharistiae participationem*, circular letter on the Eucharistic Prayers (1973)

GILH   *General Introduction to the Liturgy of the Hours* (1971)

GIRM   *General Instruction of the Roman Missal* for the dioceses of Ireland (published by Irish Liturgical Publications, 2005)

GS   Vatican II, *Gaudium et spes*, Pastoral Constitution on the Church in the Modern World (1965)

LM   *Lectionary of the Mass*, introduction (1981)

MS   *Musicam sacram*, Instruction on Music in the Liturgy (1967)

PO   Vatican II, *Presbyterorum ordinis*, Decree on the ministry and life of priests (1965)

RO   *Rite of Ordination*

SC   Vatican II, *Sacrosanctum Concilium*, Constitution on the Sacred Liturgy (4 December 1963)

CHAPTER ONE

CELEBRATING THE MYSTERY OF FAITH

The study guide begins with a short statement about the Eucharist. It should be read along with the preamble and first chapter of the General Instruction of the Roman Missal, 1-26.

In celebrating the Eucharist, the people of God assemble as the body of Christ to fulfil the Lord's command to 'do this in memory of me' (Luke 22:19). In this most sacred action of Christ and the Church, the memorial of his death and resurrection is celebrated; God is adored in spirit and in truth, the Church identifies itself with the saving Sacrifice of its Lord and, nourished by his Body and Blood, looks forward in joyful hope to sharing in the supper of the Lamb in the heavenly kingdom.[1]

At the Last Supper the Lord spoke to his disciples, took bread and wine, gave thanks, broke the bread, and gave them the Bread of life and the Cup of eternal salvation. After his resurrection from the dead, two disciples recognised his presence in these same actions: speaking, taking bread, giving thanks, breaking and sharing (see Luke 24:13-35). In the Eucharist the Church to this day makes Christ's memorial and celebrates his presence in the same sequence of actions: in the Liturgy of the Word the assembly listens with hearts burning as the Lord speaks to it again and it responds with words of praise and petition; in the Liturgy of the Eucharist it takes bread and wine, gives thanks, breaks the bread, and receives the Body and Blood of Christ.[2]

These two principal parts of the Mass are so closely connected as to form one single act of worship: the tables of God's word and of Christ's body are prepared, and from them the faithful are instructed and nourished; the spoken word of God announces the history of salvation, the Eucharist embodies it in the sacramental signs of the liturgy. In addition to these two principal parts, there are also the Introductory Rites, which prepare the people for word and Eucharist, and the Concluding Rites, which brings the people's worship to a close and sends them out to witness and service.[3]

The celebration of Mass is the action of Christ and the people of God, ministers and congregation. Within the one body of Christ there are many gifts and responsibilities. But just as each organ and limb is necessary for the sound functioning of the body (see 1 Corinthians 12), so every member of the assembly has a part to play in the action of the whole. It is therefore of the greatest importance that in all circumstances and on every occasion the celebration be so organised that priest, ministers, and faithful may all take their own part. The participation of all is demanded by the nature of the liturgy, and, for the faithful, is their right and duty by reason of their baptism.[4]

---

[1] *EM* 3, a-c
[2] *GIRM* 72
[3] *GIRM* 28, *LM* 10
[4] *SC* 14, 28; *GIRM* 16,17,18, 19, 20

- By apostolic tradition, the Church gathers on the Lord's Day to celebrate the Lord's Supper. This Sunday Eucharist, at which the entire local community assembles and in which all play their proper parts, is the primary manifestation of the local Church and, as such, the most important and normative form of Eucharistic celebration.[5] It should be in every sense inclusive and not be needlessly multiplied. The celebration of other Sacraments, when the *Roman Ritual* allows, may be accommodated within it.

- In the celebration of the Eucharist, all present, ordained or lay faithful, render the particular service corresponding to their role and function in the assembly.[6] A celebration is the work of the whole body of Christ; the ministers and other members of the assembly have a part in the action and have a contribution to make. Each of these special services is performed for the good of the whole and for the glory of God.

---

[5] *SC* 49, 106; *DD* c 3
[6] *SC* 28

CHAPTER TWO

INTRODUCING THE NEW EDITION OF *GIRM*

*This chapter introduces the **General Instruction of the Roman Missal**, giving a definition of some of the terms and, in smaller print, a more detailed account of its development from when first published in November 1969 to the new edition of March 2002.*

> ***General Instruction of the Roman Missal*** (= *GIRM*) is the introduction to the **Roman Missal**, placed at the front of the Missal we use at Mass. In the Missal we use at present it takes up sixty-three pages of small print. It is both a 'how' and 'why' document in that it explains the way Mass is celebrated but also the understanding that lies behind it. It is not just instructions and rubrics but a pastoral and theological document as clearly seen in its chapter titles. The new edition, though issued in July 2000, was published in its definitive form with the new edition of the Latin Missal on 26 March 2002, is longer and will be published in the new English Missal when the work of translation has been completed.

The following is a brief summary of its content:

Preamble
After the Second Vatican Council, a new Roman Missal was published in its Latin edition in March 1970. Some months earlier, in November 1969, the new Order of Mass had been published in Latin. This is the part of the Missal used at every Mass, the part that was called the Ordinary of the Mass as distinct from the Proper, the texts that change from day to day, like the collect or opening prayer. The introduction or *GIRM* was published also with the new Order of Mass but when it appeared with the Latin Missal in 1970, this preamble was added. There had been criticism of the Order of Mass, some claiming that it was a break with the traditional understanding of Mass. The preamble offered a defence of tradition and progress as may be seen in the headings of its main parts:

- A Witness to Unchanged Faith
- A Witness to Unbroken Tradition
- Accommodation to New Conditions

Chapter I. The Importance and Dignity of the Eucharistic Celebration
    A short introductory chapter on the centrality of the Eucharist.

Chapter II. The Structure of the Mass, its Elements and its Parts
    i   The General Structure of the Mass
    ii   The Different Elements of the Mass
    iii   The Individual Parts of the Mass
An overview and commentary of the structure of the Mass and its parts.

Chapter III. The Duties and Ministries in the Mass
  i   The Duties of those in Holy Orders
  ii   The Duties of the People of God
  iii   Particular Ministries
  iv   The Distribution of Duties and the Preparation of the Celebration
This chapter treats the different roles and ministries exercised at Mass, including 'the duties of the People of God,' the assembly.

Chapter IV. The Different Forms of Celebrating Mass
  i   Mass with a Congregation
  ii   Concelebrated Mass
  iii   Mass at which only One Minister Participates
  iv   Some General Norms for All Forms of Mass
The different forms include Mass with a congregation and concelebration. The chapter brings the reader through the Mass in detail.

Chapter V. The Arrangement and Furnishing of Churches for the Celebration of the Eucharist
  i   General Principles
  ii   The Arrangement of the Sanctuary for the Sacred Synaxis (Liturgical Assembly)
  iii   The Arrangement of the Church
General and specific principles are given on the sanctuary, the places for the congregation, choir and the location of the tabernacle.

Chapter VI. The Requisites for the Celebration of Mass
  i   The Bread and Wine for Celebrating the Eucharist
  i   Sacred Furnishings in General
  iii   Sacred Vessels
  iv.   Sacred Vestments
  v   Other things intended for Church Use
Requisites include the bread and wine used at Mass, vessels and vestments.

Chapter VII. The Choice of the Mass and its Parts
  i   The Choice of Mass
  ii   The Choice of Mass Texts
This is a technical chapter about the texts used at Mass, that is, readings and prayers.

Chapter VIII. Masses and Prayers for Various Circumstances and Masses for the Dead
  i   Masses and Prayers for Various Circumstances
  ii   Masses for the Dead
Again, this is a chapter like the previous one and includes the important statement that in preparing the celebration of Mass, the priest 'should have in mind the common spiritual good of the people of God, rather than his own inclinations.'

Chapter IX. Adaptations within the Competence of Bishops and Bishops' Conferences
This is a new chapter in the new edition of *GIRM*. It lists these adaptations but also notes the more radical adaptation called inculturation.

The new edition of *GIRM* takes account of various changes over the past twenty-five years. More recent documents are quoted, for example, a paragraph on silence given in the introduction to the Lectionary published in 1981 is quoted verbatim in *GIRM* 56 in its commentary on the Liturgy of the Word. A new Code of Canon Law, published in 1983, already created a number of amendments and these are included.

> The **Roman Missal** is the book of prayers used at Mass. The **Lectionary** is also part of the Missal, though published separately. Thus, the **Roman Missal** at present consists of several volumes, the one volume of prayer texts and the three volumes of the Lectionary.

Before Vatican II, the Missal was in one volume and it contained all the readings. But Vatican II called for 'the treasures of the Bible – to be opened up more lavishly, so that a richer share in God's word may be provided for the faithful. In this way a more representative portion of holy Scripture will be read to the people in the course of a prescribed number of years' (*SC 51*). This happened with the publication of the Lectionary and we are familiar with its Sunday structure: three readings, from Old Testament (or in Eastertime, Acts of the Apostles), New Testament and Gospel in a three year cycle.

The Missal that was published after the Council of Trent served the liturgy from 1570 until replaced by the Missal of 1970. The Missal of 1570 is sometimes called the Tridentine (that is, of Trent) Missal or the Missal of Pope Pius V, the Pope of the time. The Missal of 1970 might appropriately be called the Missal of Pope Paul VI. The 1970 date is that of the Latin edition or *editio typica*. This is the term given to the Latin edition of a liturgical book issued by Rome and used for making the translation. It was translated into English by **ICEL** and became our Mass book on the First Sunday of Lent 1975. However, the use of English (and Irish) had already begun, ten years earlier, from the First Sunday of Lent, 16 February 1965. All of the Mass was in English from 1 December 1968.

ICEL or the International Commission on English in the Liturgy is the agency of eleven Bishops' Conferences where English is spoken. It was formed during the Second Vatican Council, some weeks before the Constitution on the Sacred Liturgy, which allowed the use of the vernacular, was promulgated on 4 December 1963. Ireland has been a member of ICEL from the very beginning. ICEL is currently preparing a translation of **the new Latin Missal** issued in March 2002.

The Order of the Mass is that part of the Missal which is used at every Mass. It consists of:
- The introductory rites.
- The outline of the Liturgy of the Word. The readings, responsorial psalms, Alleluia or gospel acclamations are in the Lectionary. The Creed, in both forms (Nicene and Apostles') is given in the Order of Mass. The homily and the Prayer of the Faithful are elements of this part of Mass, though they are composed for each Mass.
- The Liturgy of the Eucharist is the major part of the Order of Mass. There are over eighty prefaces and ten Eucharistic Prayers included.
- The concluding rites, that is the Prayer after Communion, the Blessing and Dismissal.

The new Latin Missal is the third edition of the Missal which was first published on 26 March 1970. A second edition appeared in March 1975. The principal additions to the previous editions are:
- The Eucharistic Prayers that were approved later, that is, the Prayers for Reconciliation, the Prayer for Masses for Various Needs and Occasions and the Masses with Children.
- New Masses of the Blessed Virgin Mary (mostly taken from the Masses issued in 1987), other Votive Masses and Prefaces.

- The Mass prayers for saints included in the Universal Calendar since the last edition.
- Other new prayers have been added, for example, Prayers over the People for each day of Lent.

The edition of this Missal for Ireland will include the Mass prayers for the saints of the Irish Calendar.

Further reading
Dennis C. Smolarski SJ, *The General Instruction of the Roman Missal 1969-2002, a commentary,* The Liturgical Press, Collegeville, 2003.

CHAPTER THREE

THE ASSEMBLY AND ITS MINISTERS

This chapter begins with the assembly gathered for worship, gathered to give thanks and praise to God, to celebrate the Eucharist. It then explores the various ministries which serve the prayer of the assembly. Each section begins with a statement on the ministry and then lists several practical considerations.

THE ASSEMBLY

Christ is always present in the Church, particularly in its liturgical celebrations. In the celebration of the Mass, which is a memorial of the Sacrifice of the Cross, Christ is really present first of all in the assembly itself: 'Where two or three come together in my name, there am I in their midst' (Matthew 18:20).[1]

At Mass the faithful form 'a holy people, a people whom God has made his own, a royal priesthood, so that they may give thanks to God and offer the spotless Victim not only through the hands of the priest but also together with him, and so that they may learn to offer themselves. They should, moreover, endeavour to make this clear by their deep religious sense and their charity toward brothers and sisters who participate with them in the same celebration.'[2]

- The assembly is not a random group of individuals but the gathering of God's people to exercise its royal priesthood in the sacrifice of praise. Everything in the celebration is organised to encourage and foster an awareness of mutual interdependence, of common dignity and purpose.
- An attitude and a climate of hospitality and welcome to all and among all the assembly create an environment wherein liturgy can be richly celebrated.
- The dialogues between the assembly and its ministers, and the acclamations have a special value as signs of communal action and as a means of effective communication. They are not simply outward signs of communal celebration but foster and bring about communion between priest and people.[3]
- Singing is one of the most potent of all expressions of communal awareness and common purpose.[4] The assembly that finds its shared sung voice is more readily aware of its communal identity.
- Uniformity in posture and gesture likewise expresses and fosters a unity of spirit and purpose.[5]

---

[1] SC 7; GIRM 27
[2] GIRM 95; cf SC 48
[3] GIRM 34
[4] GIRM 39
[5] GIRM 42, 96

LITURGICAL MINISTERS

All members of the assembly contribute to the Eucharistic Celebration in ways appropriate to their particular order or liturgical function. By doing all and only those parts that belong to them, the ministers and other members of the assembly contribute to the participation of all and show the Church as the body of Christ, actively engaged in worship of the living God with the help of various orders and ministries.[6] The composition of the liturgical assembly, with its diversity of people and ministries, represents and reflects the nature of the Church itself.

- Liturgical celebrations require a variety of ministers. The very arrangement of the celebration in its various ministries shows that all the baptised have a place and a role in the Church – women and men, the young and old, people of every race and way of life. Through the variety of liturgical ministries in the Church, the body of Christ is built up.

- All who exercise a liturgical ministry within the assembly need proper preparation for their responsibilities. They need to have the competence to perform the particular ministry with which they have been entrusted.

- The formation of liturgical ministers is both spiritual and technical. Although this formation varies in extent and depth depending upon the nature of the particular ministry, it will normally have liturgical, biblical and technical components. Through liturgical formation ministers acquire an understanding of the Mass as a whole, with particular emphasis on the parts of the Mass for which they have responsibility. Through biblical formation they are helped to understand the cycle of Scripture readings and to perceive the revealed message of the Scriptures by the light of faith. Liturgical ministers also learn the intimate connection between the two principal parts of the Mass – the Liturgy of the Word and the Liturgy of the Eucharist. Through training in the particular skills of their ministry, they learn to make the best use of their personal gifts and strengths in order to communicate the person and message of Christ by the reverent use of word, gesture or movement.

- Opportunities should be made available periodically for liturgical ministers to pray together and for on-going renewal in their ministry. These occasions may provide for their continuing formation and for the improvement of their abilities to assist the assembly in its worship.

- The words and actions of the liturgy give verbal and bodily expression to the profound realities of God's gracious activity and the people's attitude in response to God. Equal care is therefore to be given by liturgical ministers in the exercise of their ministry to the verbal and physical elements of the liturgy. For example,
    - When speaking or singing, ministers use a natural, audible and clear voice, appropriate to the text and strive for a measured delivery.
    - By reverent posture and through graceful gesture and movement, ministers reinforce the words of the liturgy and help to elicit the response of the assembly.

- When not performing particular duties, liturgical ministers join with the rest of the assembly in their actions and responses. At these times all ministers listen, respond, and sing with the other members of the assembly and so continue to contribute to the worship of the whole body.

PRIEST CELEBRANT

In the celebration of the Eucharist, Christ is present in the person of the priest. Every authentic celebration of the Eucharist is presided over by the bishop or a priest (presbyter) presiding in the

---

[6] GIRM 91

person of Christ. The priest leads the people in prayer, in listening and responding to God's word, and in offering the Sacrifice through Christ in the Spirit to the Father. He proclaims the message of salvation in preaching and gives the Bread of eternal life and the Cup of Salvation.[7]

By the depth of the priest's prayerfulness and the dignity and humility of his bearing, the people should be able to recognise the living presence of Christ, who spoke with authority but who came not to be served but to serve. In this way the priest will be conscious that he presides over the assembly in the name of Christ and that his leadership is exercised in a ritual manner.[8]

- Through his liturgical presidency, the priest animates and encourages the participation of others. He coordinates them into one harmonious action. Rather than appropriating the functions of others, he is responsible for seeing that everything is done well.[9]
- The priest exercises his responsibility chiefly in the worthy proclamation of the presidential prayers: the Collect (Opening Prayer), the Prayer over the Offering, the Prayer after Communion, and, supremely, the Eucharistic Prayer. Presiding in the person of Christ, he addresses these prayers to God in the name not only of the assembly but of the entire people of God.[10]
- In some circumstances the priest may also facilitate the conscious participation of the assembly by brief and helpful comments and introductions, for example, at the beginning of the celebration, before the readings and the Eucharistic Prayer, or at the dismissal.[11]
- Other ministers proclaim the readings, including the Gospel, but the presiding priest ordinarily gives the Homily. Preaching is an integral part of the liturgy, particularly when the community gathers for its Sunday celebration of the Eucharist.[12] It is the first task of priests as co-workers of the bishops to preach the Gospel of God. Their role is to teach not their own wisdom but the Word of God.[13]

DEACON

The deacon, whose order has been held in high honour since the earliest years of the Church, has a principal role among the other ministers of the assembly. The deacon is ordained for service in communion with the Bishop and the college of presbyters. The deacon's service for the people of God is the *diakonia* (service) of liturgy, word and charity.[14]

- The deacon's most important function at Mass is to proclaim the Gospel reading. On occasion he may be invited to deliver the Homily and he ordinarily announces the intentions of the Prayer of the Faithful.[15]
- In the Liturgy of the Eucharist, the deacon assists in the distribution of Communion to the people, especially as ministers of the chalice. In this connection, he also prepares the table, assists the priest in receiving the gifts, prepares the chalice, elevates the chalice at the doxology, and may assist with the Breaking of the Bread before Communion.[16]

---

[7] *GIRM* 27, 92, 93
[8] *GIRM* 93
[9] cf *LM* 38.
[10] *GIRM* 30
[11] *GIRM* 31; *LM* 42
[12] *GIRM* 65-66
[13] *PO* 4
[14] *GIRM* 94; *LG* 29; *RO* 199
[15] *GIRM* 71, 94, 175, 177; *LM* 50
[16] *GIRM* 83, 94, 178, 180, 182, 284

- As servant of the assembly and its worship, the deacon assists the priest at the chair and at the altar. He is also called to give certain directions and invitations to the assembly, especially regarding movement or posture.[17] When incense is used, the deacon assists with its preparation and where indicated may incense the priest, the people and the *Book of the Gospels.*

READER

In proclaiming the word of God from sacred scripture, readers exercise their responsibility in mediating the presence of Christ. God speaks to the assembly through them, and the impact of God's message will depend significantly on their conviction, their preparation, and their delivery.[18]

The richness in the quantity and in the variety of readings in the Lectionary challenges those who are called upon to proclaim the Scriptures at Mass. Each of the individual sacred authors reflected on the meaning of God's action in history from their own perspective. They employed various literary forms to convey the message of salvation, ranging, for example, from narratives and the poetry of the psalms to prophetic oracles and parables, from theological expositions to apocalyptic visions.

- The ministry of reader requires formation and preparation that is liturgical, biblical and technical, and that is on-going.
- An awareness of the literary form of a particular reading or psalm and a knowledge of the sacred author's style will enable the reader to proclaim more fully and with greater understanding the tone and content of the text.
- It is better to have a different reader for each reading.[19] This has a number of positive consequences. It involves more people in active ministry. It assists the assembly to appreciate the genre and context of different passages of Scripture. It also allows the assembly to benefit from a different voice.
- The responsorial psalm is led by a psalmist or cantor, but, if necessary, may be led by a reader.[20]
- When there is no deacon, a reader may carry the *Book of the Gospels* before the presiding priest in the entrance procession and lay it on the altar.[21]
- When there is no deacon, the reader, after the introduction by the priest, may announce from the ambo or from another suitable place, the intentions of the Prayer of the Faithful.[22]

MINISTERS OF MUSIC

A psalmist, a cantor, an organist, other instrumentalists, a choir, and a director of music assist the assembly's full participation in singing the songs, responses, and acclamations, which are constitutive elements of the liturgy. These ministers of music exercise a liturgical function within the assembly and by their role help to add beauty and solemnity to the celebration.[23] A key to understanding this ministry is the recognition of the fundamental role of music ministers to serve the prayer of the gathered assembly.

---

[17] *GIRM* 94
[18] *GIRM* 101
[19] *GIRM* 109; *LM* 52
[20] *GIRM* 99; *LM* 22
[21] *GIRM* 118b, 119, 120,194-5
[22] *GIRM* 71,197.
[23] *GIRM* 103-104, 39-41

- All ministers of music will be aided in their ministry through the availability of training and formation. Both liturgical and musical on-going training are required.

- The psalmist has the special task of drawing the assembly into the proclamation of the Word of God in the psalm or other biblical canticle that comes between the readings by introducing the psalm responses and Gospel acclamation to the assembly, and by singing the verses of the responsorial psalm and Gospel Acclamation verses.[24] The psalmist may also introduce the antiphons to the assembly and sing the verses of the psalms used.[25] The psalmist should have the ability to sing, and a facility in correct pronunciation and diction.[26]

- The cantor's function is to lead and encourage the assembly in singing. The cantor also introduces and teaches new music to the people.[27] One person may carry out the role of the psalmist and cantor.

- The organist and other instrumentalists have the particular role of supporting and encouraging the assembly's participation through song.[28] In addition, in their own right, they can powerfully assist contemplation and express praise and a variety of human feelings before God.

- The choir remains at all times a part of the assembly. It can serve the assembly by leading it in sung prayer and by reinforcing or enhancing the song of the assembly. It can do this, for example, by sharing the singing of the verses or sections of a hymn or song alternately, by introducing a sung response or antiphon, or through harmony or other elaboration. It should never displace, or dominate the rightful song of the assembly.[29] It is appropriate for the choir alone to sing more elaborate music, for example, a motet at the Preparation of the Gifts, which can assist the prayerful reflection of the assembly.

- Even at celebrations when there is no choir, basic musical participation can be ensured by an instrumentalist and one or two cantors, or by a cantor alone. Especially through responsorial singing, such ministers can draw the people into singing together.

MINISTERS OF COMMUNION

'Since the Eucharistic celebration is the Paschal Banquet, it is desirable that the faithful who are properly disposed receive the Lord's Body and Blood as spiritual food as he commanded.'[30] If a large number are to receive communion, the priest celebrant will frequently need assistance in distributing communion, so that the Communion Rite is not unduly long. This assistance will regularly be needed when communion is given under both kinds, the form of Communion in which the Eucharistic Banquet is more clearly signified.[31]

Deacons and concelebrating priests are the ordinary ministers of Communion. Instituted acolytes, where they are available, assist as auxiliary ministers. Frequently, however, this assistance is given by extraordinary ministers of Communion, either formally commissioned for a given period or, in case of necessity, deputed by the priest celebrant.[32]

These ministers serve Christ present in the assembly by ministering his Body and Blood to their brothers and sisters. They also serve the unity of the worshipping community by taking

---

[24] *GIRM* 61-64, 102
[25] *GIRM* 48, 87
[26] *GIRM* 102
[27] *GIRM* 104
[28] *GIRM* 103, 313
[29] *GIRM* 103
[30] *GIRM* 80
[31] *GIRM* 162, 281
[32] *GIRM* 162

communion to those members who are prevented by sickness, old age, or other cause from taking part in the gathering for Mass. This is in accord with the ancient tradition whereby communion is taken directly from the Sunday eucharist to the sick and to those unable to leave their homes.

- As is true for all liturgical ministers, proper training and formation needs to be provided for those who serve in this ministry. This is both preparatory and on-going. Annual opportunities for reflection and prayer, theological input and practical training will benefit both those who engage in and those who receive from this ministry.
- When communion is being taken from Mass to the sick or those unable to leave their homes, the appropriate moment for the deacons, acolytes, or extraordinary ministers to take the pyx from the altar and leave the assembly is after the communion of the people. Alternatively, they may depart immediately after receiving communion themselves, or as part of the concluding procession of ministers.

SERVERS (other ministers)

In addition to the service of instituted acolytes, service at the altar by other ministers represents a long liturgical tradition. These servers exercise their ministry within the assembly and enhance the quality of celebration for the whole assembly by taking part in processions and by ensuring that all requisites for the celebration are available at the appropriate moments.

- Servers carry out many practical duties throughout any liturgical service. These include the following: They hold the book while the priest celebrant proclaims the presidential prayers with outstretched hands; they lead the entrance and concluding processions with the cross and candles; they escort the deacon (or priest) to the ambo and stand at his side while he proclaims the Gospel reading; they may, on more solemn occasions, accompany the procession with the gifts; they look after the thurible, prepare it for the priest or deacon, and themselves may incense the assembly and other ministers; they bring and hold such things as books, thuribles, water jug and towel, plates and dishes, and microphones.
- The number of servers will depend upon the circumstances and the tasks to be performed. Especially at large-scale celebrations, there should be an assisting minister (akin to a master of ceremonies) with responsibility for ensuring that these various tasks are properly assigned and carried out.
- Given their visibility throughout liturgical celebrations, servers also carry out another often-unnamed functions. They can serve as an example of engagement, participation and prayer for the assembly. This underlines the importance of their training and the manner in which they are to carry out their duties in the midst of the worshipping assembly.

USHERS AND MINISTERS OF WELCOME

Saint Paul instructed the assembled community to 'welcome one another as Christ has welcomed you, to the glory of God' (Romans 15:7). Indeed, it has been said that liturgy flourishes in a climate of hospitality. In the liturgical setting, therefore, it will often be appropriate for those commonly referred to as ushers to exercise this ministry of welcome. They may do this by greeting people at the door of the church, making sure they are provided with all the necessary books, music and other items for the celebration, such as candles or palms, and helping them find their places.

The people are assembled as table guests of the Lord to share in a supper as sisters and brothers. They will appreciate this more readily if they are made welcome by representatives of the community and acknowledged informally by their neighbours.

- In small and stable communities, a formal ministry of welcome may not be needed. But in larger assemblies with a more shifting attendance, special arrangements are likely to be necessary so that visitors and those unfamiliar with the community and its worship may be put at ease and drawn into the celebration.
- This is very much a ministry of presence. Ministers of welcome should be encouraged to be self-aware of the welcome with which they reach out to people.
- Ushers also help when, at any time during the celebration, members of the assembly become ill or otherwise need assistance. It is advisable for each community to discuss and determine for themselves what the correct procedures are in their own context when such a situation arises. And of course, in turn ushers need to be familiar with these emergency/first aid procedures.
- Ushers may assist with the collection and with processions.

MINISTERS OF THE ENVIRONMENT AND LITURGICAL SPACE

The environment in which the action of the assembly takes place is of huge importance. In broad terms the environment refers to the setting of the Church building in the local community. More specifically it means the character of a particular space and how it affects the action of the assembly.

At its best, the environment will serve, support and enhance the prayer of the people. It is appropriate when it is beautiful, when it is hospitable, when it clearly invites and when it needs an assembly of people to complete it.

Ministers who work to help enhance the environment include the sacristan, those in charge of flowers, those responsible for keeping the church clean and, in increasing numbers in parishes, art and environment groups.

- Elements in the environment that contribute to the overall experience include the seating arrangement, the layout of the sanctuary (i.e. ambo, altar, presider's chair) the placement of the baptistery, temporary decoration, light, acoustics, spaciousness, heat, etc.
- The sacristan arranges the liturgical books, the vestments and other things necessary in any given liturgical celebration.[33] In conjunction with parish leadership and, where present, an art and environment group, the sacristan will help ensure that what is used in the liturgy is of high quality and appropriateness.
- Florists work in tune with the liturgical year, respecting and communicating the different moods of, for example, Lent and Easter. Following the call to worship authentically, florists help ensure a living and real environment in the worship space – using flowers and plants that are real and not fake.
- Art and environment groups again work in tandem with the liturgical year and may respond to the demands placed on the environment that the liturgical year provides. Again such groups can give heed to the bigger picture of light, sound and heat in the worship space. They can also look to the quality and appropriateness of vestments, vessels and liturgical

[33] *GIRM* 105

books. They often work with symbols in the liturgy. This suggests the need for a good understanding of and respect for the primary symbols of the liturgy.

LITURGY GROUPS

In recent years there have been an increasing number of parishes that have established their own liturgy groups. These groups, made up of parishioners and parish leadership, work to prepare the liturgical celebrations of the parish.

While the vast majority of groups share a common focus on the preparation of the Sunday Eucharist, many groups will also take on board other specific tasks appropriate to their own circumstances.

The presence of liturgy groups in parishes serve as a reminder to us that liturgy is the work of all God's people. The achievement of the full, active and conscious participation of the assembly in worship is the goal of any parish liturgy group.

- Liturgy groups need the support and presence of those who will preside at the liturgies they prepare.
- To do their task well, liturgy groups require initial and on-going liturgical formation appropriate to the tasks they are setting themselves.
- Evaluation and planning are key tasks for a liturgy group. One of the many beauties of the liturgical year is that Christmas will not take us by surprise. Good planning and evaluation can lessen the load for many liturgy groups.
- Membership of liturgy groups can be drawn from a diverse grouping. One of the many things a liturgy group can do is to continually draw others into active participation so that the group is always looking beyond its own members to the wider community.

UNITY IN DIVERSITY

Clearly many ministers are needed for the vibrant and authentic celebration of the eucharist. There is a rich diversity of ministers and ministries but a unity of purpose. Among all who are involved in the preparation and celebration of the eucharist there should be harmony and diligence.[34]

It is the Body of Christ who gathers to worship and this Body is made up of many different parts and functions. The harmony and unity of the Body working together is the true worship in praise and thanksgiving of our God.

Ministers are not disparate groups but rather are intimately linked with a common purpose of serving the prayer and worship of the assembly.

- An awareness of the interdependency of all ministries and ministers needs to be instilled in the training and formation of all ministers.
- Opportunities should be provided at local or diocesan level for shared on-going formation for liturgical ministers, nurturing a sense of all ministers working together within the liturgy.

---

[34] GIRM 111

REVIEWING LITURGICAL MINISTRY IN THE PARISH

In light of what you have read in the preceding pages consider the following questions in relation to the groupings below:

- What are we doing in our own situation that supports this ministry?
- Are there any changes needed in our practice?
- What more could we do?

	Present support for this ministry	Changes needed in practice	What more could be done?
The Assembly			
Liturgical Ministers			
Priest Celebrant			
Deacon			
Reader			

This page may be copied.

	Present support for this ministry	Changes needed in practice	What more could be done?
Ministers of Music			
Ministers of Communion			
Servers			
Ushers & Ministers of Welcome			
Ministers of the Environment & Liturgical Space			

This page may be copied.

	Present support for this ministry	Changes needed in practice	What more could be done?
Liturgy Groups			
Unity among Liturgical Ministries			
Unity in Diversity			

This page may be copied.

CELEBRATING THE MYSTERY OF FAITH

CHAPTER FOUR

THE EUCHARISTIC CELEBRATION AND ITS SYMBOLS

The actions and words of the Mass are explored in this chapter. It serves as a commentary on GIRM 27-45 (pp. 20-27), 273-277 (pp. 91-94), 288-351 (pp. 99-118).

'In the liturgy, by means of signs perceptible to the senses, human sanctification is signified and brought about in ways proper to each of these signs.'[1] The entire ritual complex of actions, objects, words, and persons which constitute the symbolism of the Eucharist is integral to its effectiveness. The more clearly and powerfully each of them signifies, the more directly their effect will be perceived and experienced. Imbued by faith, words clearly proclaimed, actions deliberately and carefully performed, elements and objects authentically made and reverently handled contribute to the integrity of the liturgy and allow its symbolism to work to greater effect.

Bread and wine, breaking and sharing, eating and drinking, standing, processing, kneeling, bowing, and greeting should not need to be explained. It is in sharing and experiencing these actions in their natural integrity and consistency that their spiritual significance and effect are appropriated.

WORDS

Because the celebration of Mass is a communal activity, the priest celebrant and all others who have a ministry need to give careful thought to the different kinds of verbal communication with the assembly. Their manner of delivery will correspond to the nature or genre of the text, the scale and acoustics of the building, and the form of the celebration and the genius of the language.[2]

Sacred Scripture
Pre-eminent among the texts of the Mass are the biblical readings with their accompanying scriptural chants, for even now from the word of God handed down in writing God speaks to the people, 'and it is from the continued use of Sacred Scripture that the people of God, docile to the Holy Spirit under the light of faith, receive the power to be Christ's living witnesses before the world.'[3]

Presidential Prayers
Among the texts assigned to the priest, the Eucharistic Prayer is of first importance as the high point of the whole celebration.[4] Next in importance are the other presidential prayers: the Collect or Opening Prayer, the Prayer over the Offerings, and the Prayer after Communion.

---

[1] *SC* 7
[2] *EP* 17; *GIRM* 38
[3] *LM* 12
[4] *GIRM* 30

- These prayers are proclaimed by the priest alone, presiding in the person of Christ. They are addressed to God in the name of the entire Church and on behalf of the whole assembly.
- When the assembly is drawn into prayer by the invitation *Let us pray*, all first observe some moments of silence in which they place themselves in God's presence and make their personal petitions.
- By a most ancient tradition of the Western Church, presidential prayers have a trinitarian structure, being addressed to God (*Deus, Pater, Domine*) with and through the Son as mediator, in the unity and power of the Holy Spirit, who convokes the Church, maintains it in communion, and empowers it to pray.
- The assembly makes the presidential prayer its own and expresses its assent in the acclamation *Amen*.[5]

Common Prayers and Other Texts

The dialogues between the priest and the assembly and the acclamations are of particular importance as expressions of the prayer of the whole assembly. They are necessary as the minimum form of communal participation, whatever the form of Mass. Some texts belong to the whole assembly and as such are recited or sung, as appropriate, by the priest and assembly together. These are, for example, the acclamations, the Profession of Faith, and the Lord's Prayer.[6]

Sung Texts[7]

There are various forms of prayer that by their very nature or because of their function in the liturgy are meant to be sung.

- The psalms used in the liturgy, for example, the responsorial psalm and others designated in the *Simple Gradual*, are songs and poems of praise, thanksgiving, lament, etc. intended for singing. The opening and communion antiphons, when used, are also texts that by their very nature should be sung, along with appropriate psalm verses.[8]
- Other texts, for example, the acclamations, call for the whole assembly to take them up and voice them in song with enthusiasm.
- On Sundays, feasts, or more solemn occasions elements of the liturgy such as the Eucharistic Prayer or at least its preface may be sung, as may the other presidential prayers. Since the Eucharistic Prayer is the central prayer and high point of the Mass the singing of this prayer expresses the solemn nature of the day or occasion being celebrated.

Invitations and Introductions

At certain moments in the Mass, indicated in the rubrics and in this Introduction, the deacon or priest celebrant gives formal invitations to encourage the people's action, response, or silent preparation for prayer. In addition the priest celebrant may facilitate the people's participation by brief and well-prepared comments.[9]

- All such introductions should be adapted to the different circumstances and occasions.
- Invitations may be expressed in the words provided or in similar words.
- Invitations intended to be followed immediately by a response from the people should end with a recognisable cue, for example, *We ask this through Christ our Lord.*

---

[5] *GIRM 54*
[6] *GIRM 34-36*
[7] see chapter five Music at Mass
[8] *GIRM 48, 87*
[9] *GIRM 31; EP 14*

CELEBRATING THE MYSTERY OF FAITH

Private Prayers

Some prayers prescribed in the Mass are personal prayers of the priest or deacon. These are by their nature private and are recited inaudibly, for example, the priest's prayer of preparation before Communion.[10] This also allows the faithful to pray silently and in their own way during these moments of preparation.

MUSIC[11]

As an art placed at the service of communal prayer, music is part of the liturgical action, drawing people together and transforming them into an assembly of worshippers. For this reason music is considered integral to worship and serves a ministerial function.[12]

In all the arts the Church has admitted styles from every period, according to the proper genius and circumstances of peoples and the requirements of the liturgy. The music of our own day, from every culture and region, should also serve the assembly and its worship with due reverence and honour.[13]

In choosing music for liturgy, consideration should be given to the music itself, the text, the ritual function, and the ability of the assembly and its ministers of music. Concerning the music, factors include the quality of composition, its ability to express the tone, content, and form of a text (for example, an acclamation or a hymn), likewise the ease with which it can be remembered and sung. A text may be prescribed (for example, the *Sanctus*) or freely chosen (for example, a song for the Communion procession). Regarding the ritual function, music may be an accompaniment to an action (for example, a procession) or a constitutive element of the rite itself (for example, the memorial acclamation).[14]

- The primary sources for the texts of liturgical music are Scripture and the prayers of the liturgy.
- Music is provided in the Missal as a model, especially when singing will be unaccompanied. Composers may create suitable settings appropriate to the culture and traditions of the people.
- Many forms or types of music are employed in the liturgy according to the nature of the various components of the rites, for example, the responsorial form, acclamations, responses, and hymns.

Instrumental music may be employed to lend a particular tone to the celebration and especially to create an atmosphere conducive to recollection, stillness, or silent prayer. Many different instruments may be used to effect.

While music is integral to every liturgical celebration, not every liturgy is celebrated with the same degree of solemnity. Sundays and Solemnities enjoy pride of place and demand greater preparation. All celebrations are prepared in the light of the community's needs and resources.

---

[10] *GIRM* 33
[11] see chapter five Music at Mass
[12] *SC* 112
[13] *SC* 112, 123
[14] *GIRM* 39-41

It is important that the music chosen reflects the nature of the season or occasion, that it contribute to developing a stable repertoire, and, if it will be used regularly, that it be strong enough to bear repetition.

The selection of music begins with the liturgical texts themselves. Priority should be given to singing the constitutive parts of the Mass in preference to hymns, and among these parts priority should be given to the responsorial psalm, to the acclamations before the Gospel and within the Eucharistic Prayer (the *Sanctus*, memorial acclamation, and *Amen*), and to the dialogues between the priest and the people (for example, the preface dialogue and the final dismissal).[15]

SILENCE

Silence is, as in all communication, a most important element in the communication between God and the community of faith. Its purpose is to allow for the voice of the Holy Spirit to be heard in the hearts of the people of God and to enable them to unite personal prayer more closely with the word of God and the public voice of the Church.[16] During liturgical silence all respond in their own way, recollecting themselves, pondering what has been heard, petitioning and praising God in their inmost spirit.[17]

Liturgical silence is not merely an absence of words, a pause, or an interlude. It is a stillness, a quieting of spirits, a making of time and leisure to hear, assimilate, and respond. Any haste that hinders reflectiveness should be avoided. The dialogue between God and the community of faith taking place through the Holy Spirit requires intervals of silence, suited to the assembly, so that all can take to heart the word of God and respond to it in prayer.[18]

- At the beginning of the rite of blessing and sprinkling of water, the people pause to ask for God's blessing on the water as a sign of baptism. In the Penitential Act, they pause to remember their sinfulness and the loving-kindness of God in Christ. At the Collect (opening prayer), they put themselves and their deepest needs and desires before God. After the readings and Homily, they savour God's word, ponder it in their hearts like Mary (see Luke 2:19), and apply it to their lives. Before Communion, they compose themselves to receive the Lord, and afterwards praise and pray to God in their hearts.[19]
- Liturgical silence is a corporate activity shared in by all present, by which all support and sustain each other in profound prayerful solidarity. It demands a stillness and prayerful concentration, which the priest celebrant and all ministers can help to bring about.
- Structurally, liturgical silence is indispensable to the rhythm of a balanced celebration. Without it the celebration can become perfunctory in its haste or burdensome in its unrelieved sound and song.

---

[15] *LM 19-20; GIRM 40; MS 7, 29*
[16] *GILH 202; EP 18*
[17] *EP 18*
[18] *LM 28, GIRM 56.*
[19] *GIRM 45*

MATERIALS AND OBJECTS

Materials and objects used in the Eucharist are to be 'truly worthy and beautiful,' authentic in their noble simplicity, and well adapted to sacred use.[20] The greatest care and sensitivity are necessary, even in the smallest matters, to achieve 'a noble simplicity and elegance.'[21]

- *The Place of Worship* is the pastoral directory on the building and reordering of churches, issued by the Episcopal Commission for Liturgy and its Advisory Committee on Sacred Art and Architecture, published by Veritas and the National Centre for Liturgy.

Altar

'The altar on which the Sacrifice of the Cross is made present under sacramental signs is also the table of the Lord to which the People of God is called together to participate in the Mass, as well as the centre of the thanksgiving that is accomplished through the Eucharist.'[22]

- A white cloth should be on the altar, its shape, size and decoration in keeping with the altar's design.[23]
- Only what is required for the celebration of Mass should be placed on the altar. The *Book of the Gospels* may be placed on the altar from the beginning of Mass until the proclamation of the Gospel. At the presentation of the gifts, the following are placed on the altar – the paten and chalice, corporal, purificator and Missal. They are removed from the altar at the purification of vessels after Communion. Microphones should be arranged discreetly.[24]
- At least two candles may be placed on or around the altar, suited to the design of the altar and sanctuary and not interfering with the people's view of what takes place at the altar.[25]
- Moderation should be observed in the decoration of the altar. Flowers should not be placed on the mensa (table) of the altar. The altar should not be decorated with flowers during Lent and with a moderation suited to the season during Advent.[26]

Bread and Wine

The very nature of sacramental symbolism demands that the elements for the Eucharist be recognisable, in themselves and without explanation, as food and drink.

- Bread made only from wheat flour (and by tradition of the Western Church unleavened) should 'have the appearance of food.' In colour, taste, texture and smell it should be identifiable as bread by those who are to share it. This is just as necessary when small individual breads are used.
- Wine should be natural and pure, from the fruit of the grape, and free from any foreign substance.[27] To be seen and recognised for what it is and what it signifies, it can help greatly if the wine is brought to the altar in clear glass containers and is of a sufficiently rich colour to be clearly distinguishable from water.

---

[20] *GIRM* 288, 325, 236
[21] *GIRM* 351
[22] *GIRM* 296
[23] *GIRM* 304
[24] *GIRM* 306
[25] *GIRM* 307
[26] *GIRM* 305
[27] *GIRM* 322

Vessels

Vessels for the eucharistic elements should be made of worthy and durable materials, their form in keeping with local culture and with their function in the liturgy.[28]

- The fundamental eucharistic symbolism of the many sharing in the one bread and one cup is more clearly expressed when all the bread is contained in a single vessel and all the wine in one chalice. Additional vessels may be necessary for the distribution of Communion and may be brought to the altar at the Breaking of the Bread.
- Vessels for the Body of Christ preferably have the form of plates or shallow bowls rather than of chalices or reliquaries. Chalices for the blood of Christ need to be large enough to be shared, easily handled between minister and communicant, and easily tilted by the communicant for the purpose of drinking.
- A suitable jug and basin may be used for the washing of the priest's hands. The water presented with the gifts for mixing with the wine is not appropriate for this purpose. Generous quantities of water and a towel will be necessary if the priest is to do more than wet the tips of his fingers.

Ambo

When the Scriptures are read in the church, God speaks to the assembly, and in the proclamation of the Gospel Christ himself is present in his word: it is Christ himself who speaks.[29] The place from which the Scriptures are proclaimed, the ambo, is regarded as the 'table of God's word' and is therefore a symbol of the surpassing dignity of that word.[30]

In accord with its dignity, the ambo is used exclusively for the proclamation of God's word in the Scriptures, including the singing of the responsorial psalm; the elucidation and application of the word in the Homily and the Prayer of the Faithful; and also the Easter proclamation (Exsultet).[31] The ambo should not be used for music practices or announcements.

Chair

Christ is present in the person of his minister who presides at the liturgy. The chair stands as a sign of the priest celebrant's office.[32] It symbolises unity, leadership, and service to the gathered assembly. Its position allows the priest to be seen easily and heard by all in the assembly.[33]

- From the chair the priest leads the Introductory and Concluding Rites and presides over the Liturgy of the Word. He may also give the Homily at the chair, sitting or standing, and say the Prayer after Communion.[34]
- When priest and ministers move from chair, to ambo, to altar, the different parts of the Mass are more clearly distinguished, and the presence of the Lord in word and sacrament is more effectively conveyed.

Cross

The Paschal Mystery celebrated in the eucharistic liturgy was accomplished through the Crucifixion and Resurrection. Christians glory in the cross of the Lord (see Galatians 6:14). As a constant reminder of the cost of salvation and the symbol of Christian hope, the cross should be

---

[28] *GIRM 328-332*
[29] *SC 7*
[30] *GIRM 29, 309; LM 32*
[31] *LM 33*
[32] *GIRM 310*
[33] *GIRM 27, 310*
[34] *GIRM 124, 165; LM 26*

visible to the entire assembly during the Eucharist. It may be carried in procession, or there may be a fixed cross on or near the altar.[35] Care should be taken not to multiply crosses in the place of worship and so detract from the effect of this symbol of the Paschal Mystery.

Books

Books used in the celebration of the Eucharist serve to communicate God's presence to us in the word or to signify the Church's response to God in praise and adoration. In both capacities they facilitate the action of Christ in the Church.[36]

- Books from which the word of God is proclaimed are treated with veneration. They need to be of large size, strong binding, and noble design. Other books, including the *Missal*, while worthy, need not draw attention to themselves. Pamphlets and leaflets detract from the visual integrity of the total liturgical action and should never be used by ministers as they exercise their particular ministry.

Vesture

Vestments serve several functions in the celebration of the Eucharist. As festive clothing, for example, they suggest the ritual and solemn character of the eucharistic banquet, and as insignia, they identify the specific function or ministry in the assembly of those who wear them.[37]

- The garment common to all ministers is the alb, which can express unity and enhance the visual dignity of the celebration. Its form and design should complement the ritual and festive character of the celebration.
- The chasuble, worn with alb and stole, is the proper vestment of the presiding priest. It may be made from either natural or synthetic fabrics that are worthy and beautiful. Beauty should derive from the quality and cut of the fabric as much as from its ornamentation.[38]
- The variety in the colour of the sacred vestments is to give effective and outward expression to the specific character of the mysteries of faith being celebrated and to a sense of Christian's life's passage through the course of the liturgical year.[39]
- Concelebrating priests wear either a chasuble and stole, or a stole alone, over the alb. Vestments that differ in size, shape, and ornamentation can obscure unity, emphasise individualism, and detract from the presidential role of the presiding priest.
- The deacon wears an alb, stole, and dalmatic; but the dalmatic may be omitted.[40]

Incense

Incense has been used since before Christian times both as a sign of respect and honour and as a symbol of prayer rising before God. Incense suggests both the otherness of the transcendent God and the cloud which symbolised God's glory and presence in the midst of the Israelites. It can contribute powerfully to a sense of mystery. As a sweet-smelling aroma, it represents the prayers of the Church rising before God as an acceptable oblation (see Psalm 141:2; Revelation 8:4).

- Incense, which when burning, appeals to our sight and our sense of smell should be used in amounts sufficient to be readily seen and smelled.
- In the introductory rites, incense may be carried in the entrance procession and used at the veneration of the altar. In the Liturgy of the Word, it may be carried in the Gospel

---

[35] *GIRM* 122, 308
[36] *LM* 35
[37] *GIRM* 335
[38] *GIRM* 337, 343, 344
[39] *GIRM* 345-6
[40] *GIRM* 119b, 336, 338

procession and used to venerate the *Book of the Gospels*. In the Liturgy of the Eucharist, it may be used at the preparation of gifts to honour the gifts of bread and wine and the altar and to acknowledge the presence and action of Christ in the priest celebrant and the other members of the assembly. It may also be used at the showing of the Body and Blood of the Lord after their consecration.[41]

- The use of incense at any of these points, or at all, is optional, and its use at any one point does not necessitate its use at all the others. It is used in order to express the solemnity of a particular celebration or to enhance a particular moment within a celebration.

- Before or after an incensation, a profound bow is made to the person or object that is incensed, except in the case of the incensation of the altar and the gifts for the Sacrifice of the Mass. The thurible is swung back and forth three times (only) for the incensation of the Blessed Sacrament, the gifts for the Sacrifice of the Mass, the altar cross, the *Book of the Gospels*, the Paschal candle, the priest and the people. The offerings may be incensed with three swings of the thurible or by making the sign of the cross over them.[42]

- The thurible is swung back and forth twice (only) for the incensation of relics and images of the Saints exposed for public veneration. These are incensed only at the beginning of the celebration, after the incensation of the altar.[43]

- The priest incenses the altar with single swings as he walks around it.[44]

GESTURE AND POSTURE

The active participation of the faithful is first of all internal in that their thoughts reflect what they hear, do, and say during the liturgy. It is also external in that through their outward bearing and gestures they express their inner participation in the liturgy. The ritual interplay of the internal and external elements of the liturgy conveys the transcendence and the immanence of the living God whom the assembly worships.[45]

Since worship engages people fully, in every aspect of their being, they worship God with their bodies and feelings as well as their minds and spirits, with their hands and feet as well as their eyes and ears. The non-verbal elements of the liturgy reinforce the spoken word and, at times, express what cannot be articulated in words. Because of their power, the gestures and postures of the liturgy deserve as much care as its words.

The people are called as members of an organic whole, not as disparate individuals. A Christian assembly that worships 'with one heart and soul' (Acts 4:32) adopts a common posture as a sign of its unity. Such common posture both expresses and fosters the mind and spiritual attitude of those taking part.[46]

- Actions done together by the whole assembly express its unity and cohesion in the body of Christ. Some actions and gestures are performed by the whole community together, for example, making the Sign of the Cross, standing to pray, sitting to listen, bowing to show reverence, moving forward to present and receive, exchanging the sign of peace.

---

[41] *GIRM 276*
[42] *GIRM 277*
[43] *GIRM 277*
[44] *GIRM 277*
[45] *MS 15*
[46] *GIRM 42*

- Other actions are performed by the priest celebrant or another minister, for example, praying with hands raised and outstretched, blessing with hands extended over the people, showing the consecrated elements to the people, and the Breaking of the Bread.

Posture

There is a common understanding of the significance of the postures of standing, sitting, and kneeling. One rises to greet people, to honour someone important, to express readiness for action, or when seized with excitement. In Christian liturgical tradition, standing is the basic posture of an Easter people lifted up to greet its risen Lord. The assembly stands at Mass, for example, during the proclamation of the Gospel reading.[47]

One sits to listen, to rest, to watch. At Mass it is appropriate, for example, to sit during the Homily and at the Preparation of the Gifts.[48] This recalls the posture of the disciple who sits at the feet of the Master (see Luke 10:39).

One kneels as a human gesture of submission. In Christian tradition, kneeling is an acknowledgement of one's creatureliness before God. It can signify penitence for sin, humility, reverence, and adoration.[49]

Other Postures and Gestures

Other gestures employed in the celebration of the Mass include bowing, genuflecting, kissing and striking the breast. Each of these gestures has had a natural significance in human experience and in Christian liturgical tradition, but this may vary considerably according to culture and epoch.

Bowing may be seen as a natural and gracious sign of respect.

- A bow of the head is made at the name of Jesus and when the three Divine Persons are named together, at the name of the Blessed Virgin Mary and of the saint in whose honour Mass is being celebrated.[50]
- A bow of the body or a profound bow is made to the altar and in the Creed at the words, *By the power of the Holy Spirit... and was made man.* The priest makes a number of additional bows as indicated in the Missal.[51]

Genuflecting is an ancient gesture of fealty, reverence, and adoration.

- As a sign of adoration, genuflection is therefore reserved for the Most Blessed Sacrament. A genuflection is also made to the Holy Cross from the Celebration of the Lord's Passion on Good Friday until the Easter Vigil.
- A genuflection is made at the words of the Creed, *By the power of the Holy Spirit... and was made man* on the Solemnities of the Annunciation of the Lord and the Nativity of the Lord.
- If the tabernacle with the Blessed Sacrament is located in the sanctuary, the priest, the deacon, and the other ministers genuflect when they approach the altar and leave the sanctuary, but not during the celebration of Mass itself.

---

[47] *GIRM* 43
[48] *GIRM* 43
[49] *GIRM* 43
[50] *GIRM* 275a
[51] *GIRM* 275b
[52] *GIRM* 274
[53] *GIRM* 274

- At other times, all who pass before or come into the presence of the Most Blessed Sacrament genuflect, unless they are part of a procession.[52]
- A genuflection is made by bending the right knee to the ground.[53]

Kissing is a more intense sign of reverence and respect.

- The altar, as the table of the Lord, is venerated with this sign of reverence by the priest at the beginning of Mass and, as a rule, at the end of Mass.

Processing is the formal movement of people from one place to another.

- There are several processions at Mass: the priest celebrant and ministers at the beginning and end of Mass, the gospel procession, the procession with gifts and offerings and the procession of people at Communion.

The Sign of Peace is the greeting and gesture of peace and reconciliation after the Lord's Prayer and before the Breaking of Bread. It recalls Christ's admonition to be reconciled before presenting our offering of sacrifice (Matthew 5:23).

- The gesture of peace that has become customary in Ireland is a handsake or handclasp.

The Sign of the Cross is the sign of belief in the saving death and resurrection of Christ.

- The Mass begins and ends with the sign of the cross. The Gospel is greeted with each person marking forehead, lips and heart with the sign of the cross. Many people make this gesture after receiving Communion.

CHAPTER FIVE

MUSIC AT MASS

In order to make this chapter more complete, some paragraphs from chapters three and four are repeated here.

As an art placed at the service of communal prayer, music is part of the liturgical action, drawing people together and transforming them into an assembly of worshipers. For this reason music is considered integral to worship and serves a ministerial function.[1]

In choosing music for liturgy, consideration should be given to the music itself, the text, the ritual function and the ability of the assembly and its ministers of music. Concerning the music, factors include the quality of composition, its ability to express the tone, content, and form of a text (for example, an acclamation or a hymn), likewise the ease with which it can be remembered and sung. A text may be prescribed (for example, the *Sanctus*) or freely chosen (for example, a thanksgiving song after Communion). Regarding the ritual function, music may be an accompaniment to an action (for example, a procession) or a constitutive element of the rite itself (for example, the memorial acclamation).[2]

- The primary sources for the texts of liturgical music are Scripture and the prayers of the liturgy.
- Music is provided in the Missal as a model, especially when singing will be unaccompanied. Composers may create suitable settings appropriate to our traditions and culture.
- Many forms or types of music are employed in the liturgy according to the nature of the various components of the rites, for example, the responsorial form, acclamations, responses, and hymns.

Instrumental music may be employed to lend a particular tone to the celebration and especially to create an atmosphere conducive to recollection, stillness, or silent prayer. Many different instruments may be used to effect.

While music is integral to every liturgical celebration, not every liturgy is celebrated with the same degree of solemnity. Sundays and Solemnities enjoy pride of place and demand greater preparation. Other celebrations are planned in the light of the community's needs and resources.

It is important that the music chosen reflect the nature of the season or occasion, that it contribute to developing a stable repertoire, and, if it will be used regularly, that it be strong enough to bear repetition.

The selection of music begins with the liturgical texts themselves. Priority should be given to singing the constitutive parts of the Mass in preference to hymns, and among these parts priority

---

[1] *SC* 112
[2] *GIRM* 39-41

should be given to the responsorial psalm, to the acclamations before the Gospel and within the Eucharistic Prayer (the *Sanctus*, Memorial Acclamation, and *Amen*), and to the dialogues between the priest and the people (for example, the preface dialogue and the final dismissal).[3]

When choosing music, ask the following questions:
- Does the music reflect the season or the occasion?
- Does it contribute to developing a stable repertoire?
- Is it strong enough to bear repetition?
- Can it be easily remembered and sung?
- Has attention been given to instrumental music?
- Has attention been given to the place of silence?

The most important questions are:
- Does the music chosen respect the priorities of music in the liturgy, for example, have the more important pieces been attended to in the first place?
- Has the place of the congregation been respected throughout the choice of music?

The answers to these questions should be guided by the next section of this chapter. It treats the music of the Mass in order of importance and also indicates the role of the congregation in each piece.

Sung Texts

There are various forms of prayer that by their very nature or because of their function in the liturgy lend themselves to being sung. It is important that when sung the settings used are appropriate to the prayer form and text.

- The psalms used in the liturgy, for example, the responsorial psalm and others designated in the *Simple Gradual*, are songs and poems of praise, thanksgiving, lament and so on, intended for singing. The opening and communion antiphons, when used, are also texts that by their very nature should be sung, along with appropriate psalm verses.[4]
- Other texts, for example, the acclamations, call for the whole assembly to take them up and voice them in song with enthusiasm.[5]
- On Sundays, feasts, or more solemn occasions elements of the liturgy like the Eucharistic Prayer or at least its preface may be sung as may the other presidential prayers. Since the Eucharistic Prayer is the central prayer and high point of the Mass, the singing of this prayer also expresses the solemn nature of the day or occasion being celebrated.

Eucharistic Prayer

We begin with the Eucharistic Prayer as it is the centre and summit of the entire celebration.[6]

Beginning with the Dialogue and ending with the Great Amen, the Prayer has a unity that should be expressed musically. The presider prays the Prayer in the name of the assembly. The whole prayer has been given musical settings by many composers and a simple setting is given in the *Missal*. The Preface, which expresses the element of thanksgiving in a special way, ought to be

---

[3] *LM* 19-20; *GIRM* 40; *MS* 7, 29
[4] *GIRM* 48, 87
[5] *GIRM* 35, 40
[6] *GIRM* 78

sung, at least, on special occasions. The acclamations are of particular importance and should be sung if possible.

Dialogue

The singing of the Dialogue at the beginning of the Prayer captures the sense of the Prayer as that of the entire community.[7]

Sanctus Acclamation

This acclamation is an integral part of the Eucharistic Prayer. It belongs to priest and people together.[8] Of its very nature it is a song and should be sung, even if on occasion the preface is not sung. Choir or cantor parts may also be sung if they facilitate and enhance the congregation's participation.

- The text of the *Sanctus* should be that of the *Missal*.

Memorial Acclamation

The Memorial Acclamation of the people in the Eucharistic Prayer confesses the Church's belief in the central mystery of our faith, the Paschal Mystery of Christ's death, resurrection, and presence among his people.

- The Memorial Acclamations provided are not specific to the four Eucharistic Prayers; each may be used with any of the prayers.
- As acclamations they are intended to be sung.
- The texts of the acclamations should be those of the *Missal*.

Amen

We commonly refer to the doxology by its opening words *Through him, with him, in him*. The Eucharistic Prayer ends with this expression of the glorification of God in the doxology, literally a word of prayer. When sung by the presider, it enables the congregation to sing its Great Amen.

- The profound importance of the assembly's ratification and acclamation can be difficult to bring out in the one short word *Amen*. It should be sung, or at the very least spoken loudly, both at the Sunday and weekday celebrations. Musical settings which prolong the *Amen* or repeat it or even intersperse it between the phrases of the Doxology sung by the priest can all help the assembly to experience and express its true power.
- At all Masses, we should try to have the Great Amen sung, even if nothing else might be sung.

Gospel Acclamation

The *Alleluia* or Gospel Acclamation is an acclamation which expresses the people's greeting of the Lord and their faith in his presence as he addresses them in the Gospel reading.[9]

The Gospel Acclamation has traditionally accompanied the Gospel Procession, in which the *Book of the Gospels* is carried to the ambo accompanied by lights and incense.

- As an acclamation, the *Alleluia* or Gospel acclamation is sung by everyone present. The verse may be sung by cantor or choir (or even recited).[10]

---

[7] see *GIRM* 35
[8] *GIRM* 79b
[9] *GIRM* 62; *LM* 23
[10] *GIRM* 62, 63; *LM* 23

- The *Alleluia* or Gospel acclamation looks forward to the Gospel reading. It is not a response to the previous reading, from which it is separated by a distinct pause.
- The assembly stands while the procession moves to the ambo and the *Alleluia* is sung.
- Where there is only one reading before the Gospel, the *Alleluia* or the verse before the Gospel may be omitted if it is not sung.[11]

Responsorial Psalm

The Responsorial Psalm follows the First Reading and is an integral part of the Liturgy of the Word. After hearing and taking to heart God's word, the assembly responds with words which are themselves God-given. This response, the Psalm, holds great liturgical and pastoral importance because by this use of the word of God meditation on the word of God is fostered.[12]

The psalms have been used to give prayerful expression to the faith and feelings of God's people over the centuries. They were used by Christ himself in prayer. In these words of wonder and praise, repentance and sorrow, hope and trust, or joy and exultation the Church now responds to God's word. The psalms in the *Lectionary* have been selected to help the assembly to meditate on and respond to the word that has just been proclaimed.

The assembly is to be helped and encouraged to discern God's word in the psalms, to adopt them as their own prayer, and to experience them as the prayer of the Church.

- The psalms, the songs and hymns of Israel, are normally sung. This may be done in a variety of ways. The preferred form is responsorial, in which the psalmist or cantor sings the verses and the whole assembly takes up the response. In the direct form, which is also permitted, there is no intervening response and the cantor, or the whole assembly together, sings the verses consecutively.[13]
- But if other ways of singing or sharing the psalms are appropriate, such as the use of a sung response with a recitation of the text, these too may be used, so that the people's participation may be facilitated by every means.[14]
- Even when it is impossible to sing the psalm, it may be possible to support and enrich its recitation with instrumental music. Psalms should always be recited in a manner conducive to meditation.[15]
- The common Responsorial Psalms, and responses provided in the *Lectionary* for various seasons and days (see volume I, pp 949-963), may be used instead of the one assigned for the day, if that choice would facilitate sung participation.[16]
- The Responsorial Psalm is normally sung from the ambo.[17]

Entrance Song

The purpose of the entrance song or chant is to open the celebration, foster the unity of those who have gathered, introduce their thoughts to the mystery of the liturgical season or festivity, and accompany the procession of the priest and ministers.[18] The choice of song should be in keeping with this understanding.

- The entrance song is normally sung entirely, or in part, by the people.

---

[11] *GIRM* 63
[12] *GIRM* 61
[13] *LM* 20
[14] *LM* 21
[15] *LM* 22
[16] *GIRM* 61; *LM* 89
[17] see *GIRM* 309
[18] *GIRM* 47

Communion Song

The Communion of priest and people is traditionally accompanied by the singing of a psalm with a simple congregational refrain. The antiphon provided may be replaced by a psalm or suitable liturgical song. The text and the music should express the union in spirit of communicants and highlight the 'communitarian' nature of the procession to receive Communion.[19]

- The communion song begins immediately after the common recital of *Lord, I am not worthy.*
- So as not to encumber the assembly with books or scripts during the procession, the song may be led by cantor or choir and include a repeated response or refrain from the assembly.
- Although several Communion songs may be sung in succession, depending on the length of Communion, it may be preferable to balance singing with periods of silence or instrumental music.
- Many traditional Eucharistic hymns were composed for Benediction of the Most Blessed Sacrament. They concentrate on adoration rather than on the action of communion and may not be appropriate as communion songs.

Kyrie

The *Kyrie* is an ancient chant by which the assembly acclaims the Lord and pleads for mercy. It is used to conclude the first form and second form of the Penitential Act and is included in the third form of the Rite. The Roman Church adopted it from the Eastern liturgies, where it formed the response to various litanies of intercession. It may be used in English or in the original Greek.[20]

- It is by nature a chant and, when used, is normally sung by all, with the choir or cantor having a part in it.

Gloria

The *Gloria* is one of the Church's most ancient hymns. In the West its use was originally restricted to the opening of only the most solemn eucharistic celebrations.

- The *Gloria* is by nature a festive hymn and is normally sung entirely, or in part, by the people.
- The *Gloria* is sung on Sundays outside the seasons of Advent and Lent, on Solemnities and Feasts, and at special celebrations of a more solemn character. The text of this hymn may not be replaced by any other text.[21]

Breaking of the Bread

During the Breaking of the Bread, the *Agnus Dei* is sung or said. The assembly calls on Jesus as the Lamb of God (see John 1:29, 36) who has conquered sin and death (see 1 Peter 1:18; Book of Revelation 5:6, 13:8). The *Agnus Dei* is a litany-song intended to accompany the action of breaking and may therefore be prolonged by repetition. It loses its entire purpose if a perfunctory Breaking of Bread is already completed before the *Agnus Dei* has even begun.

Song of Praise after Communion

When Communion is completed, the whole assembly may observe a period of total silence. In the absence of all words, actions, music, or movement, a moment of deep corporate stillness and

---

[19] *GIRM 86*
[20] *GIRM 52*
[21] *GIRM 53*

contemplation may be experienced. Such silence is important to the rhythm of the whole celebration and is welcome in a busy and restless world.

- As an alternative or addition to silent contemplation, a psalm or song of praise may be sung. Since there should normally have been singing during Communion, silence may be more desirable.[22]

Sequence
Sequences are provided in the *Lectionary* for Easter Sunday, Pentecost, The Body and Blood of the Lord and Our Lady of Sorrows (15 September). They are optional, except on Easter Sunday and Pentecost. The sequence is sung before the *Alleluia*.[23]

Recessional Song
The recessional procession may be accompanied by a psalm or song, a seasonal hymn, appropriate instrumental music, or silence.

Other Parts of the Mass
Other parts of the Mass may also be sung. For example, the choir may sing an appropriate song or motet at the preparation of the gifts, many congregations sing *Ár nAthair*, and when water is blessed at the beginning of Mass, the congregation might be invited to sing a baptismal acclamation. On some occasions, the response to the intentions of the Prayer of the Faithful may be sung.

When the priest sings the greeting or the blessing at the end of Mass, there is a sung congregational response: *And also with you*. Similarly, if the priest sings the collect, prayer over the gifts and the prayer after communion, the congregation sings the *Amen*.

After choosing music, ask the following questions:
- Have the priorities, as in the order of listing the sung texts above, been respected?
- What role has been given to the cantor?
- What part has the choir to play in the choices made?
- Is the participation of the congregation respected?

Ministers of Music
A psalmist, a cantor, an organist, other instrumentalists, a choir, and a director of music assist the assembly's full participation in singing the songs, responses, and acclamations, which are constitutive elements of the liturgy. These ministers of music exercise a liturgical function within the assembly and by their role help to add beauty and solemnity to the celebration.[24] A key to understanding this ministry is the recognition of the fundamental role of music ministers to serve the prayer of the gathered assembly.

- All ministers of music will be aided in their ministry through the availability of training and formation. Both liturgical and musical on-going training are required.

---

[22] *GIRM* 45, 88, 164
[23] *GIRM* 64
[24] *GIRM* 103-104, 39-41
[25] *GIRM* 61-64, 102
[26] *GIRM* 48, 87
[27] *GIRM* 102

CELEBRATING THE MYSTERY OF FAITH

- The psalmist has the special task of drawing the assembly into the proclamation of the Word of God in the psalm or other biblical canticle that comes between the readings by introducing the psalm responses and Gospel acclamation to the assembly, and by singing the verses of the responsorial psalm and Gospel Acclamation verses.[25] The psalmist may also introduce the antiphons to the assembly and sing the verses of the psalms used.[26] The psalmist should have the ability to sing, and a facility in correct pronunciation and diction.[27]

- The cantor's function is to lead and encourage the assembly in singing. The cantor also introduces and teaches new music to the people.[28] One person may carry out the role of the psalmist and cantor.

- The organist and other instrumentalists have the particular role of supporting and encouraging the assembly's participation through song.[29] In addition, in their own right, they can powerfully assist contemplation and express praise and a variety of human feelings before God.

- The choir remains at all times a part of the assembly. It can serve the assembly by leading it in sung prayer and by reinforcing or enhancing the song of the assembly. It can do this, for example, by sharing the singing of the verses or sections of a hymn or song alternately, by introducing a sung response or antiphon, or through harmony or other elaboration. It should never displace, or dominate the rightful song of the assembly.[30] It is appropriate for the choir alone to sing more elaborate music, for example, a motet at the Preparation of the Gifts, which can assist the prayerful reflection of the assembly.

- Even at celebrations when there is no choir, basic musical participation can be ensured by an instrumentalist and one or two cantors, or by a cantor alone. Especially through responsorial singing, such ministers can draw the people into singing together.

---

[28] *GIRM* 104
[29] *GIRM* 103, 313
[30] *GIRM* 103

Towards Congregational Singing

The following points may help those preparing the liturgy to improve congregational singing:

1. People sing short refrains much more easily than long verses.
2. Some music will need to be repeated from week to week if the congregation is to grow accustomed to singing.
3. The more important chants of the Mass have popular settings which in fact use refrains, for example, the Gospel Acclamation, the Memorial Acclamation, the Great Amen, the Responsorial Psalm. It is wise to begin working on congregational singing by focussing on just one or two of these for a few weeks. As texts are well known, hymnals or sheets are not normally necessary.
4. Pick very easy settings to start.
5. A certain minimum number of pieces should be repeated for a month, a season, or even the whole year.
6. It is quite permissible, for the sake of congregational singing, to use the same Responsorial Psalm over a period of weeks. Obviously the psalm will need to be carefully chosen if this approach is adopted. The Lectionary offers a selection of common psalms in vol. I, pp 949-963.
7. People are more inclined to sing if there is a cantor who is able to rehearse them briefly in one or two pieces before Mass and can continue to encourage them to sing during the celebration itself. This person need not be a good singer, but must be a good encourager!
8. If a leaflet is being used, those parts which are to be sung by everyone should be clearly marked. When the word 'choir' appears after a title the congregation is less likely to join in. Words such as 'all sing' are helpful before the appropriate refrains.
9. If people do not know the words of a particular piece off by heart, it is not fair to expect them to sing unless a text is provided for them.
10. The entrance song should normally be one in which everyone can join with ease, otherwise a 'passive' tone will be set for all the remaining music of the liturgy.
11. It takes a long time to educate a 'passive' congregation into active participation in music and some persistence is often needed. It may take a year before real progress is made!

Resources

Several hymnals, published over the years, are standard resources. Irish published collections include: *Veritas Hymnal, Alleluia! Amen!, Hosanna!, Seinn Alleluia 2000, In Coelo, Feasts and Seasons.* Well known British publications include *Laudate, Celebration, Liturgical Hymns Old and New. Gather*, published in USA, is widely used.

Two complete settings of the Responsorial Psalms for every Sunday have been composed by the late Fintan O'Carroll and by Margaret Daly-Denton in the collection, *Cantate*.

A setting of *Entrance Antiphons for the church year* has been composed by John McCann.

There are many Mass settings with the Eucharistic Prayer acclamations, the Gospel Acclamation and other parts of the Mass.

Most hymnals include some Gregorian chant which holds pride of place because it is proper to the Roman Liturgy.[31] A more complete repertoire is found in *Jubilate Deo*.

---

[31] *SC* 116; *MS* 50; *GIRM* 41

MUSIC PLANNING SHEET

Sunday/Feastday: _____

Cantor: _____

Organist/Accompanist/Music Group: _____

First Reading	Responsorial Psalm	Second Reading	Gospel

Entrance Song	
Kyrie	
Gloria	
RESPONSORIAL PSALM	
GOSPEL ACCLAMATION	
Prayer of the Faithful	
Preparation of the Gifts	
SANCTUS	
MEMORIAL ACCLAMATION	
GREAT AMEN	
Lord's Prayer	
Agnus Dei	
Communion Song	
Song of Praise after Commuinion	
Recessional Song	

This page may be copied.

CHAPTER SIX

THE ORDER OF MASS

This chapter is a study of the Order of Mass. It explores the various parts or elements that make up the Mass.

- The chapter is based on the relevant articles of the *General Instruction on the Roman Missal*. Prior to and within each section below, the reader will find the corresponding articles and pages of the *GIRM*. It is hoped that readers will have access to a copy of this instruction.

- Certain elements within the rites will be highlighted or spotlighted – it is impractical to do a comprehensive treatment of every aspect of the rite in this guide. Again, access to the *GIRM* will make it possible to further augment study of the various elements within the Eucharistic celebration.

- What follows presupposes an understanding that music is integral to the liturgy. Chapter five 'Music at Mass' in this guide is a necessary companion to what follows. References to music are indicated as ♪ with the chapter five page in the margin as ♪ p 00.

- Liturgical prayer is embodied prayer. Posture within the liturgy is about more than decorum or convention but has a key role in our experience of communal prayer. Therefore you will notice boxed references to posture when appropriate in the side column.

INTRODUCTORY RITES

GIRM **background reading:** 46-54 (pp 28-31) & 120-127 (pp 57-59)

PURPOSE: In the introductory rites the assembly is called together in Christ and established again as the Church. The risen Lord is present in the midst of the assembly, which becomes visible as the body of Christ. Thus, the assembly itself is the first instance of Christ's presence in the liturgy. The function of these rites is to enable the community, coming together from a multiplicity of concerns and a variety of ways of life, to become aware of itself again as a gathered community, alert and ready to listen to the word and to celebrate the sacrament.

STRUCTURE

Entrance procession

The assembly's worship begins with the opening song and procession, which help to create an ambience of celebration, a sense of identity, and an awareness of the mystery being unfolded.

Greeting

After making the sign of the cross together, the priest and people exchange formal greetings as a mutual acknowledgement and evocation of the presence of Christ in their midst and as a prayer for his sustaining power.

Opening Rite – The Penitential Act or Rite of Blessing and Sprinkling of water

The Penitential Act may take several forms that we are familiar with in the Missal. It may be replaced by the Rite of Blessing and Sprinkling of water, particularly appropriate during the Easter season. The choice may be made on the basis of the liturgical season, the feast, the particular occasion, or on the basis of the circumstances of the assembly that gathers for the celebration.

The third form of the Penitential Rite is a litany of praise, addressed to Christ our redeemer (and not a litany of our sins!). The invocations, or those modelled on them, focus on Christ and his mercy.

Kyrie Eleison

After the Penitential Act, the *Kyrie* is always begun, unless it has already been included as part of the Penitential Act.

♪ p. 41

Gloria

The Gloria is sung or said on Sundays outside of Advent and Lent, Solemnities, Feasts and on special occasions. Its text should not be replaced by any other text.

♪ p. 41

Collect

The Collect (or opening prayer) begins with an invitation to pray. Therefore, a brief silence is observed. The Collect ends with a full trinitarian conclusion.

Spotlight on...

Entrance Procession

The entrance procession of ministers through and from the assembly expresses visibly the relationship of the priest celebrant and the other ministers to the congregation. It can take different forms – it may be simple or more solemn or festive. *GIRM* 120 outlines the order of the procession in detail.

- The thurifer carrying a thurible with burning incense, if incense is used.

- The ministers with candles, and between them the cross-bearer.
- Other servers.
- A reader (or deacon) who may carry the *Book of the Gospels*.
- The priest celebrant.

The priest and ministers make a profound bow, as a sign of reverence, on reaching the altar. If the tabernacle is in the sanctuary, they genuflect, though ministers who are carrying a liturgical object do not bow or genuflect.

After venerating the altar, the priest celebrant, on more solemn occasions, incenses the cross and the altar, walking around the latter.

After the procession and the reverencing of the altar, the priest and deacon proceed to the chair. From there the priest greets the people and leads the opening rite.

Spotlight on...

Greeting

The Greeting of the people is the first dialogue between priest and people. The greeting and response should be both warm and reverent. Casual and personalised greetings that emphasise a merely human exchange and obscure the mystery of Christ's presence and action are inappropriate.

However, a brief and well-prepared introduction can help to create the appropriate atmosphere and give tone and orientation to the entire celebration.

- At this point strangers, guests and special groups may be briefly welcomed.
- When significant numbers of children are present, they may be acknowledged and addressed directly at this point.
- Though the introduction will normally be the function of the priest, on occasion it may be fitting for the deacon or some other member of the assembly to do this.

LITURGY OF THE WORD

GIRM **background reading:** 55-71 (pp 31-37) & 128-138 (pp 59-61)

PURPOSE: The Mass is made up of the Liturgy of the Word and the Liturgy of the Eucharist, which are so closely linked as to form one act of worship. By hearing the word proclaimed in worship, the faithful enter into the unending dialogue between God and God's people, a dialogue sealed in the sharing of the Eucharistic food. The proclamation of the word is thus integral to the Mass and at its very heart. In this dialogue with the Lord, the people listen to the word, reflect on it in silence, respond to it in song, assimilate it, and apply it to their lives. Moved by it, they profess their faith and intercede for the needs of the Church and the world.

STRUCTURE

Biblical Readings

The proclamation of the Gospel reading is the high point of the Liturgy of the Word. The other readings in their established sequence from the Old and New Testaments prepare the assembly for this proclamation.

The people sit for these readings and the responsorial psalm.

When a prayerful silence is observed before or after a reading, the whole assembly is to take part in it. The reader does not move to or from the ambo during the period of silence.

The Liturgy of the Word may, when it would be helpful, be introduced by a brief word on the background of the readings. Such comments, whether from the priest celebrant or another minister, should always be succinct and well prepared.

Responsorial Psalm

The responsorial psalm follows the first reading and is an integral part of the Liturgy of the Word. The assembly is to be helped and encouraged to discern God's word in the psalms, to adopt them as their own prayer, and to experience them as the prayer of the Church.

♪ p. 40

Gospel Acclamation

The *Alleluia* or Gospel acclamation is an acclamation which expresses the people's greeting of the Lord and their faith in his presence as he addresses them in the Gospel reading.

♪ pp. 39-40

Gospel Reading

Because the proclamation of the Gospel reading is the high point of the Liturgy of the Word, it is distinguished from the other readings by special marks of honour. The people stand to hear the Gospel reading and acclaim Christ present and speaking to them. Servers with candles may stand on each side of the ambo, and the book may be incensed before the text is proclaimed. If the

The people stand.

Book of the Gospels is used, it is carried in procession from the altar to the ambo.

Homily

The people sit.

The homily is an integral part of the liturgy and a necessary source of nourishment for the Christian life. By means of it the mysteries of faith and the guiding principles of Christian living are expounded, most often from the Scriptures proclaimed but also from the other texts and rites of the liturgy.

Profession of Faith (Creed)

The people stand for the Creed and the Prayer of the Faithful.

In the profession of faith the people respond and give their assent to the word of God heard in the readings and the homily. Before they celebrate the mystery of faith in the Eucharist, they call to mind the rule of faith in a formulary approved by the Church.

Prayer of the Faithful

Enlightened and moved by God's word, the assembly exercises its priestly function by interceding for all humanity. The Church prays not just for its own needs but for the salvation of the world, for civil authorities, for those oppressed by any burden, and for the local community, particularly those who are sick or who have died.

Spotlight on...

Homily

In the readings God's word is accessible to people of every age and condition. But the Homily as a living explanation of the word increases its impact by assisting the faithful to assimilate it and apply it in their lives. It leads them from contemplation of the word to a profound appropriation of the mystery of Christ and his Sacrifice in a more wholehearted celebration of the Eucharist and in their daily lives.

If it is to fulfil its purpose, the Homily must be the fruit of meditation, carefully prepared, and in length, style and content sensitively adapted to the needs and capacities of all present. This may well be more easily achieved if the priest prepares the Homily in shared reflection and prayer with members of the congregation. Some parishes already have established this practice of reflection and prayer on the following Sunday's readings in order to help in this Homily preparation.

- On Sundays and holy days of obligation there must be a Homily at all Masses celebrated with a congregation; it may not be omitted without a serious reason.
- For the benefit of those people who are regular participants, and because it is an integral part of the liturgy, a Homily is appropriate at almost all Masses with a congregation. It is strongly recommended on

---

the weekdays of Advent, Christmas, Lent, and Easter and on other occasions when people come in considerable numbers.

- The priest celebrant ordinarily gives the Homily. A deacon or, at a concelebration, one of the concelebrating priests may be invited to preach. At Masses with children, where few adults are present, if the priest lacks the necessary skills to communicate with children he may ask another adult to speak to the children after the Gospel.

- The priest celebrant gives the Homily while standing or sitting at his chair or from the ambo. In particular circumstances the homilist may need to approach closer to the congregation in order to communicate effectively.

- The custom of beginning and ending the Homily with the Sign of the Cross arose when the sermon was somewhat detached from the liturgy of the Mass. The practice is not now advised.

- It is most appropriate that a period of silence follow the Homily, so that the people may take the word of God to heart and prepare a response to it in prayer.

- If catechumens are present, they may be kindly dismissed before the Profession of Faith in order to go and reflect together on the word proclaimed. Texts for the dismissal are provided in the *Rite of Christian Initiation of Adults*.

A Catechumen is a person preparing to become a Christian through the sacraments of Initiation: Baptism, Confirmation and Eucharist.

RCIA (Rite of Christian Initiation of Adults) is the process by which the Church brings new adult members into its communal life.

Spotlight on...

Prayer of the Faithful

'The joy and hope, the struggle and anguish of the people of this age and especially of the poor and those suffering in any way are the joy and hope, the struggle and anguish of Christ's disciples.'[1] Thus, even though the intercessions may be quite concrete or particular in content, they should always look beyond the concerns of the local assembly to the needs of the whole Church and of the wider world. As such, they are a sign of the communion of the particular assembly with all other assemblies and with the universal Church.

The priest celebrant directs the prayer from the chair. He briefly invites the people to pray, and at the end he draws their intercessions together in a brief concluding prayer. A deacon, another minister, or members of the assembly propose the intentions at the ambo or some other suitable place. After each intention, the faithful respond by silent prayer or a common response or both. They affirm the concluding prayer of the priest with their *Amen*.

[1] *GS* 1.

- The Prayer of the Faithful (general intercessions) is ordinarily included in all Masses.

- Both the priest's introduction and the proposed intentions are addressed to the assembly, not to God. They are invitations or biddings to the faithful, who then pray for the suggested intention in the silence of their hearts and in a common petition. Hence the practical need for silence within these intentions.

- These intentions should be short, clear and objective enough for the faithful to comprehend and respond to them without difficulty.

- The response they seek to evoke is petition rather than praise, thanksgiving or repentance.

- On particular occasions, when other sacraments or particular rites are celebrated in conjunction with the Mass (for example the Rite of Marriage or Funeral Rites) the range of intentions may be more closely concerned with the occasion; but even then, the intercessions should always include some general or universal intentions.

- For each intention, the invitation to pray and the response may be sung or the entire intention may be sung or even spoken while music is played.

- Those who propose the intentions return to their places only after the completion of the concluding prayer, led by the priest celebrant.

LITURGY OF THE EUCHARIST

GIRM background reading: 72-89 (pp 38-46) & 139-165 (pp 61-68)

PURPOSE: At the Last Supper, Christ instituted the sacrifice and paschal meal that make the sacrifice of the cross present in the Church. From the days of the apostles the Church has celebrated that sacrifice by carrying out what the Lord did and handed over to his disciples to do in his memory. Like him, it has taken bread and wine, given thanks to God over them, broken the bread, and shared the bread and cup of blessing as the body and Blood of Christ (see 1 Corinthians 10:16). The Church's Eucharist, in all its rich variety of forms and traditions, has always retained this basic shape: the taking of the elements of bread and wine in the preparation of the gifts, the act of thanksgiving in the eucharistic prayer, the breaking of the bread, the giving and sharing of the body and blood of Christ in communion. In the Liturgy of the Eucharist we remain faithful to this pattern of worship handed on to us through tradition.

STRUCTURE
Preparation of the Gifts
The purpose of this rite is to make the altar, the gifts that are placed on it, and the assembly ready for the Eucharistic offering which is to follow.

♪ p. 42

The people are seated.

The Church encourages the faithful to bring forward, and even to provide, the bread and wine through which Christ's offering will be made present, together with money and other gifts for the sustenance of Christ's body, especially in the poor and needy.

The taking of bread and wine at the beginning of the Liturgy of the Eucharist is not itself the sacrifice or offering but a preparation for the Eucharistic Prayer and for communion. It is the Eucharistic Prayer that is the great act of blessing and thanksgiving and which constitutes the Church's memorial offering of Christ's sacrifice.

It is most desirable that the people, just as the priest is bound to do, receive the Lord's Body from hosts consecrated at the same Mass and, when permitted, receive under both kinds. Care should be taken to prepare the bread and wine that is needed at each Mass.

Prayer over the Offerings
The prayer over the gifts concludes the preparation of the gifts and points forward to the Eucharistic Prayer.

After concluding the prayer over the gifts, the priest should make a distinct pause to make clear that the preparation of the gifts (the 'taking') is complete and that the Eucharistic Prayer (the 'giving thanks') is now about to begin.

The Eucharistic Prayer
The Eucharistic Prayer, the centre and summit of the entire celebration, sums up what it means for the Church to celebrate the Eucharist. It is a memorial proclamation of praise and thanksgiving for God's work of salvation, a proclamation in which the Body and Blood of Christ are made present by the power of the Holy Spirit and the people are joined to Christ in offering his sacrifice to the Father. The Eucharistic Prayer is proclaimed by the priest celebrant in the name of Christ and on behalf of the whole assembly, which professes its faith and gives its assent through dialogue, acclamations and the *Amen*. Since the Eucharistic Prayer is the summit of the Mass, its solemn nature and importance are enhanced when it is sung.

The people stand for the Preface, from its opening dialogue until after the Sanctus. Generally they kneel for the rest of the Eucharistic Prayer, though in special circumstances, they may stand.

The Communion Rite
The eating and drinking together of the Lord's body and blood in a paschal meal is the culmination of the Eucharist. The assembly is made ready to share in this banquet by a series of rites that lead from the Eucharistic Prayer directly to the communion.

Each of these rites (the Lord's Prayer, sign of peace, breaking of bread) is important in itself. Yet in the context of the whole celebration, they constitute together a transition from one high point, the Eucharistic Prayer, to another, the sharing in communion. The impression should not be given that they are of greater significance than the thanksgiving that precedes them or the eating and drinking which follows them.

The Lord's Prayer

Because of its themes of daily bread and mutual forgiveness, the Lord's Prayer has been used in all liturgical traditions as a most appropriate preparation for communion, 'so that what is holy may be given to those who are holy'.[2]

The people stand.

As the family prayer of all God's children, the Lord's Prayer belongs to the whole assembly. When sung, it is sung by everyone together.

The embolism, enlarging upon the last petition of the Lord's Prayer itself, is said by the priest alone and is concluded by the assembly.

The Rite of Peace

The rite of peace is not an expression merely of human solidarity or good will; it is rather an opening of ourselves and our neighbours to a challenge and a gift from beyond ourselves. In this exchange the assembly acknowledges the insistent gospel truth that communion with God in Christ is enjoyed in communion with our sisters and brothers in Christ. It is a profession of faith that we are members, one with another, in the body of Christ.

All the members of the assembly, ministers and people, turn to those immediately around them to share a sign of peace – which should be sufficiently strong and expressive in itself to not need explanatory song or commentary.

If extraordinary ministers are to assist at communion, it is desirable that they come to their place on the sanctuary by the end of the exchange of peace. They do not stand around the priest celebrant, as concelebrants would.

The Fraction

This characteristic action of Christ at the feeding of the multitude, at the Last Supper, and at his meals with the disciples after the resurrection, was so central to the Eucharist that it seems to have given its name to the entire celebration in the days of the apostles.

Just as many grains of wheat are ground, kneaded, and baked together to become one loaf, which is then broken and shared out among many to bring them into one table-fellowship, so those gathered are made one body in the one bread of life which is Christ (see 1 Corinthians 10:17). Thus, the natural, the practical, the symbolic, and the spiritual are all inextricably linked in this most powerful symbol.

[2] *GIRM 56*

Communion[3]

Faithful to the Lord's command to his disciples to 'Take and eat', 'Take and drink', the assembly completes the Eucharistic action by eating and drinking together the elements consecrated during the celebration.

In light of this command, it is most desirable that the faithful share the chalice. Drinking at the Eucharist is a sharing in the sign of the new covenant (see Lk 22:20), a foretaste of the heavenly banquet (see Mt 26:29), a sign of participation in the suffering Christ (see Mk 10:38-39). Provision should be made for this fullest form of participation in accord with the conditions laid down by the Bishop.

When communion is being taken from Mass to the sick or those unable to leave their homes, the appropriate moment for the deacons, acolytes, or extraordinary ministers to take the pyx from the altar and leave the assembly is after the communion of the people. The priest celebrant can formally send these ministers in procession from the Church in the name of the community – reminding the assembly of absent and sick brothers and sisters and of their duty of care for the sick in their midst.

Alternatively, they may depart immediately after receiving communion themselves, or as part of the concluding procession of ministers.

When communion is completed, the whole assembly may observe a period of total silence. Such silence is important to the rhythm of the whole celebration and is welcome in a busy and restless world.

The people stand.

Prayer after Communion

Then a final presidential prayer brings to a close the communion rite. In it the community of faith asks that the spiritual effects of the Eucharist be experienced in its members' lives.

Spotlight on...

Preparation of the Gifts

The altar: The first focus is on the altar and its preparation to receive the gifts that will be presented. Up to this point in the celebration, with the exception of its veneration at the beginning, the altar had not been a focus of attention. It remains almost bare and unused during the liturgy of the word, which is centred at the ambo. Now the setting is prepared for the sacred meal.

- Everything indicates that a new and important stage of the liturgy is

---

[3] See section on Ministers of Communion in Chapter three for procedures at communion time for these ministers

about to commence. A corporal is laid out of sufficient size to accommodate all the vessels that may be brought to the altar now and at the time of communion.

- The corporal, purificators, and Missal are all needed for the celebration. However, they are not themselves offerings or gifts and so are not brought up in the procession of gifts. They should be brought reverently but without ceremony from a side table, along with the chalice if it is to be prepared at the altar.
- Since these are preparatory tasks, a deacon, acolyte, server or other member of the assembly, carries them out.

The gifts: It is one of the Church's most ancient customs that the people themselves provided the materials for the Eucharist. They also brought other foodstuffs to be blessed for their own use and for the poor. The rite of carrying up the gifts continues the spiritual value and meaning of this ancient custom. This is also the time to bring forward money or gifts for the poor and the Church.

The Procession with the Gifts is a powerful expression of the assembly's participation in the Eucharist and in the social mission of the Church. It is an expression of the humble and contrite heart, the dispossession of self that is a necessary prerequisite for making the true offering which the Lord Jesus gave his people to make with him. The Procession with the Gifts expresses also our eager willingness to enter into the 'holy exchange' with God: 'accept the offerings you have given us, that we in turn may receive the gift of yourself.'[4]

- The *Collection* of money takes place first. As an integral part of the Eucharistic liturgy since apostolic times, its purpose and value will be better appreciated if, after the Prayer of the Faithful, the priest celebrant, ministers, and people all sit and wait while the collection is taken and then made ready with the other gifts for the procession. The collection is not taken during the Profession of Faith or the Prayer of the Faithful, nor does it continue during the Prayer over the Offerings or the Eucharistic Prayer. Music or song may begin with the collection and continue during the procession of gifts; it should continue at least until the gifts have been placed on the altar.
- The *bread and wine* are carried in the procession in vessels that can be seen by all the assembly. So far as possible, the bread and wine should each be contained in a single vessel, so that priest and people may be seen to be sharing the same food and drink in the sacrament of unity that is the Eucharist.
- *Members of the Congregation* carries the gifts of bread, wine and money forward. It is more expressive of the assembly's identification

---

[4] see *Roman Missal*: 29 December, Prayer over the Gifts.

with the gifts if the procession passes right through the assembly. The priest, who may be assisted by the deacon and other ministers, accepts the gifts. The collection of money and other gifts are deposited in a suitable place. The priest places only the vessels containing the bread and wine on the altar.

- *Gifts in kind and other real gifts* for the poor, besides money, are appropriate, but not token items that will be retrieved and returned to ordinary use after the celebration. (Very often these tokens are expressive of identity so that if used they are better suited to an opening procession.)

- *The use of Music* at this stage is explored in chapter five.

- *The priest celebrant holds the vessel* containing the bread slightly above the altar and blesses God. He places the bread on the altar. He then holds the chalice in the same way, blesses God, and places the chalice on the altar. Since the taking of bread and wine is expressed primarily by the action, normally both formularies will be uttered inaudibly. If there is no music, the priest celebrant may say them aloud. In this case, the people respond with the acclamation: *Blessed be God forever.* The two formularies are a unit; it should never happen that one is said inaudibly, the other aloud.

- *The preparation of the chalice* is the function of the deacon. When no deacon is present, the priest celebrant prepares the chalice. The one who prepares the chalice says the prayer *By the mystery* inaudibly. The chalice may be prepared at the side table before the bread and wine are placed on the altar.

- Incense may be used at the preparation of the gifts to honour the elements and to acknowledge the presence and action of Christ in the priest celebrant, the ministers and the rest of the community:

    - The priest incenses the gifts and the altar. The deacon or other minister incenses the priest and the rest of the assembly.

    - When incensed, the members of the assembly and other ministers stand.

Spotlight on...

Eucharistic Prayer

The Eucharistic Prayer is proclaimed over the people's gifts. It has a rich and varied tradition. Through this prayer the Church gives praise and thanks for God's holiness and justice and for all God's mighty deeds in creating and redeeming the human race. These deeds reached their climax in the incarnation, life, death and resurrection of Jesus Christ.

♪ pp. 38-39

In the Eucharistic Prayer:
- the mystery of Christ's saving death, and resurrection is recalled;

- the Last Supper is recounted;
- the memorial Sacrifice of his Body and Blood is presented to the Father;
- and the Holy Spirit is invoked:
  - to sanctify the gifts and
  - transform those who partake of them into the Body of Christ,
  - uniting the assembly and the whole Church and family of God, living and dead,
  - into one communion of love, service, and praise to the glory of the Father.

The following Eucharistic Prayers are provided for use in Ireland:
- *Eucharistic Prayers I-IV* are the principal prayers and are for use throughout the liturgical year.
  - Eucharistic Prayer II has a proper preface, based on the rest of the prayer, which is said to follow an ancient Roman model. But other prefaces may be substituted for it, especially those that similarly present the mystery of salvation.
  - Eucharistic Prayer IV has a fixed preface and so may be used only when a Mass has no preface of its own and on Sundays in Ordinary Time.
- *Eucharistic Prayers for Masses of Reconciliation I and II* express thanksgiving in the context of the reconciliation won by Christ. They are particularly appropriate for use during the season of Lent and may be used at other times when the mystery of reconciliation is reflected in the readings or others texts of the Mass or is the reason for a particular gathering of the faithful. They may be used with any preface of a penitential character.
- *Eucharistic Prayers for Masses with Children I-III.* These may be used at Masses when children constitute a significant proportion of the assembly. These texts are for the purpose of enhancing the participation of children in this central prayer of the Mass and of preparing them to take full part in Masses with adults. These prayers, with their variety of acclamations, will be most effective in engaging the children when sung. The three prayers use different levels of language.
  - Prayer I may be more suitable for those only recently introduced to the Eucharist.
  - Prayers II and III may be more appropriate as children grow in sacramental awareness and in familiarity with the Eucharistic liturgy.
  The texts are rich in catechetical themes which may be drawn upon when preparing children for the Eucharistic celebration and as the basis for reflecting with them afterward on, for example:
  - the nature of the Eucharist as thanksgiving for creation and salvation;
  - the role of the Spirit;

- the real presence of Christ in the Eucharist and the Church;
- the concepts of Sacrifice, Sacrament and meal.

- *The Eucharistic Prayers for Masses for Various Needs and Occasions* may be used in various circumstances. Its proper prefaces and closely related intercessions make it particularly suited to use with the formularies of the Masses for Various Needs and Occasions, which do not have their own proper prefaces.

There are four forms of this Eucharistic Prayer:

- The Church on the way to unity
- God guides the Church on the way of salvation
- Jesus, way to the Father
- Jesus, the compassion of God

Spotlight on...

Breaking of the Bread

Both the bread and its breaking must be truly authentic and recognisable in order for the meaning and symbolism of this rite to be perceived. The Eucharistic Bread is to 'have the appearance of food'[5] and is made so that it can be broken and distributed to at least some of the members of the assembly. This authenticity lies at the heart of vibrant and meaningful Eucharistic celebrations.

The premise that the faithful are not ordinarily to be given Communion from the tabernacle is another corner stone of authentic liturgy. We receive back what we have given in this liturgy, but what we have given returns to us as the Body of Christ.

- When for genuine pastoral reasons, for example, the late arrival of unexpected numbers, the bread consecrated at the Mass must be supplemented with the Body of the Lord consecrated and reserved in the tabernacle after a previous Mass, this may be brought reverently but without ceremony from the tabernacle to the altar at the Breaking of the Bread.
- The priest celebrant, if necessary with the help of a deacon or a concelebrant, does the Breaking of Bread with dignity and deliberation. It begins after the exchange of peace is completely finished, and the attention of the assembly is again focused on the action taking place at the holy table.
- The regular use of larger hosts will foster an awareness of the fundamental Eucharistic symbolism in which the whole assembly, priest and people, share in the same bread. At every Mass at least one

---

[5] *GIRM* 321

large Host is broken into several portions. The priest consumes one of these portions; the rest are distributed to at least some other members of the assembly.

- If additional patens are needed for the distribution of the Body of the Lord they are to be brought to the altar at this time.
- During the Breaking of the Bread, the *Agnus Dei* is sung or said. The assembly calls on Jesus as the Lamb of God who has conquered sin and death. The *Agnus Dei* is a litany-song intended to accompany the action of breaking and may therefore be prolonged by repetition. It loses its entire purpose if a perfunctory Breaking of Bread is already completed before the *Agnus Dei* has even begun.

♪ p. 41

Spotlight on...

Distribution of Communion

♪ p. 41

The communion procession is a central element of the Communion Rite. It expresses:
- the humble patience of the poor moving forward to be fed;
- the alert expectancy of God's people sharing the Paschal meal in readiness for their journey;
- the joyful confidence of God's pilgrim people on the march toward the promised land.

Our sign of reverence for the Eucharist is best expressed in the action of walking solemnly in procession in respectful readiness to receive communion.

- There should be a sufficient number of ministers to assist in the distribution of Communion. This will normally mean two ministers of the Precious Blood to each minister of the Body of the Lord.
- It is most desirable that all who minister the Eucharist take full part in the entire liturgy and share in the proclamation of the word, the Eucharistic prayer, and the consummation of the celebration in Eucharistic communion.
- The consecrated Bread may be received in the hand. The choice whether to receive in this manner is the prerogative of the communicant.
- The parish priest or priest celebrant should see to the full and proper implementation of Communion under both kinds in accordance with the provisions made by the Conference of Bishops. Even when Communion is given under both kinds, however, the communicant may refrain from drinking from the chalice.
- By tradition the deacon ministers the chalice. Beyond this, no distinctions are made in the assignment of the consecrated elements to particular ministers for distribution. Therefore, when a concelebrating priest or priests and other ministers share in the

distribution, the elements are not assigned on the basis of any distinction between ministers, cleric or lay, male or female. All may minister either element. This avoids any seeming depreciation of one or other of the consecrated elements or of a particular ministry.

- If and when communion is received by intinction the following formula is said, 'The Body and Blood of Christ', and the communicant responds, 'Amen'. In this case it is the minister, and not the person receiving, that carries out the action of dipping the host in the chalice and giving it to the communicant on the tongue.

- *Reception of Communion for People with Coeliac condition:* It is estimated that 1 in 200 people suffer from this condition in Ireland. People have varying degrees of tolerance – some can tolerate the ordinary altar breads, some can tolerate low-gluten hosts and some have a zero tolerance and will only be able to receive from the cup. (Note: Some hosts labelled 'Gluten-free' are more properly called 'low-gluten'.) This zero tolerance of gluten presents a huge difficulty for people who wish to receive and who find that the chalice is not available to them.

  It is recommended that people with Coeliac condition make themselves known to the parish so that they can be facilitated to receive in whatever form they wish – from the cup or, in some cases, in the form of low-gluten hosts.

  Parishes are also encouraged to provide a notice board sign in the church alerting people with this condition to the possibilities for reception – an active gesture of welcome and inclusion.

CONCLUDING RITES

GIRM background reading: 90 (p 46) & 166-170 (pp 68-69)

PURPOSE: After the communion rite, the Mass closes with a brief concluding rite. Its purpose is to send the people forth to put into effect in their daily lives the Paschal Mystery and the unity in Christ, which they have celebrated. They are given a sense of abiding mission. This mission calls them to witness to Christ in the world and to bring the gospel to the poor.

STRUCTURE
Note: When another liturgical rite is to follow immediately, for example, the final commendation at a funeral, the entire concluding rite is omitted because these other rites will have their own form of conclusion.

Brief Announcements

Just as the introductory comments by the priest at the beginning of the celebration may help the assembly to a better appreciation and experience of the mysteries celebrated in the Eucharist, so also the pastoral announcements at the end may help the people to make the transition from worship into renewed Christian witness in society.

Greeting and Blessing

The greeting *The Lord be with you* helps the assembly to focus attention again on the prayerful aspect of blessing.

The people stand.

The priest celebrant may use either a solemn blessing or a prayer over the people. He is encouraged to give a more solemn form of blessing on Sundays and Holydays.

All these various forms of blessing conclude always with the trinitarian formulary, during which the priest with his right hand traces the sign of the cross over the members of the assembly as they make the sign of the cross on themselves.

Dimissal

The dismissal sends the members of the congregation forth to praise and bless the Lord in the midst of their daily responsibilities.

It is the deacon's role to say or sing the dismissal, which should be done in a way that invites the people's response.

The response *Thanks be to God* is a statement of grateful praise for encountering the risen Christ in the assembly's worship.

Beginning at the Easter Vigil and up to and including the Second Sunday of Easter, the double *Alleluia* is added to the dismissal and response. It is also added on Pentecost.

The words of dismissal should reflect the sacredness of the ritual. Casual remarks or secular forms of farewell are out of place as they detract from the dignity of the rite.

Recessional Procession

The priest celebrant and deacon kiss the altar if they are near it at the time of the dismissal or pass it as they leave.

♪ p. 42

After giving proper reverence to the altar, the ministers ordinarily leave in the same order in which they entered at the beginning of the celebration.

If they have not left earlier, ministers who are to bring communion to the sick may take their place immediately before the concelebrants in the procession.

Further reading

Dennis C. Smolarski SJ, *How Not to Say Mass*, Paulist Press, New York and Mahwah, 2003. A guide to liturgical principles and practice revised in accord with the new edition of *GIRM*.

Catholic Bishops' Conference of England and Wales, *Celebrating the Mass, a pastoral introduction*, CTS, London. Like this guide, *Celebrating the Mass* uses much of the material prepared in the 1990s referred to in the foreword, p. 7, and adapted for England and Wales.

John F. Baldovin SJ, *Bread of Life, Cup of Salvation, Understanding the Mass*, Sheed & Ward Book, Rowman & Littlefield, Lanham, 2003. A commentary on the theology, history and liturgy of the Mass.

Edward Foley, *From Age to Age*, Liturgy Training Publications, Chicago, 1991. A comprehensive account of how Christians have celebrated the Eucharist.

PASTORAL ADAPTATION OF THE CELEBRATION

*The final three chapters of the **General Instruction of the Roman Missal** are concerned with adapting the celebration of the Eucharist to diverse cultural and pastoral circumstances. These adaptations take place, principally, at two different levels, that of the bishops (either in their dioceses or together at Conference level) and that of the local or parish level.*

1. WHY MAKE ADAPTATIONS?

Participation

The reform of the liturgy that was mandated by the fathers at the Second Vatican Council was guided by a number of principles, central to them being the 'full, conscious, and active participation in liturgical celebrations called for by the very nature of the liturgy'.[1]

Such participation permits the prayer and petition of the assembly and its individual members find a place in its common prayer. It allows the community to minister to itself through various persons – its own members – who, in the name of all, build up the Body of Christ in its act of service: visit the dying; minister as readers; bring communion to the sick; chant the psalm between the readings; welcome members of the living Body of Christ as they come to church and see to the needs of the elderly, the infirm or people with young children; serve as extraordinary ministers of the Eucharist; or minister as musicians and singers so as to enable the song of the entire assembly.

In order that the 'full, conscious, and active participation' called for by the Council be facilitated, it is required at times that the customs and needs of the community which is celebrating the liturgy be taken into consideration. The purpose of this is never to enhance or promote cultural or local mores, but rather to help the community in its task of offering its prayer of intercession, praise and glory to God.

The Idea of Adaptation

The Liturgy Constitution speaks about the need to adapt the liturgy to local needs, saying that the Church 'has no wish to impose a rigid uniformity in matters that do not affect the faith or the good of the whole community'.[2] The Constitution sets out two different directions in which this might happen.

- ***Rome to the Local Church.*** In this instance the various liturgical books prepared by Rome set out the type of adaptations which bishops (at both diocesan and Conference levels) can make.[3] The Introduction to every liturgical book now contains a section which invites the Local Church to make decisions about how it might adapt the liturgy to its own particular needs and customs.

---

[1] *SC 14, GIRM 386*
[2] *SC 37*
[3] *SC 38-39*

- *Local Church to Rome.* This kind of adaptation – of a more radical nature – happens when a Local Church wants to introduce adaptations or changes to the prayers or rites that have *not been* foreseen by Rome.[4]

GIRM concludes with a chapter which lists various decisions and adaptations which can be made in relation to the celebration of the Eucharist by bishops and the Conference of Bishops. It also deals with procedures to be followed when a Conference wishes to initiate modifications not foreseen by Rome. This chapter is new and reflects norms already set out in *Varietates legitimae, Instruction on the Roman Liturgy and Inculturation* issued in 1994.

2. MAKING ADAPTATIONS AT PARISH AND LOCAL LEVEL

GIRM and this study guide present the celebration which the Church regards as the norm and model of the Eucharist: the principal Sunday celebration of the parish community. This celebration assumes the availability of all necessary resources, the participation of an assembly, and a range of ministers and musicians.[5]

But if every Mass were celebrated in identical form and with the same degree of solemnity, then the Sunday celebration would cease to be truly pre-eminent. The revised liturgical books clearly presuppose that every celebration, in whatever circumstances, will fully take account of the needs, capacities, and situation of the community which assembles for it.[6] The fact that local events and pastoral needs create particular circumstances which vary, and that each parish has diverse resources at its disposal means that adaptations must be made.

The liturgical celebrations of culturally and ethnically mixed groups require special attention. Weekday Masses, celebrations with smaller groups, celebrations outside churches or chapels, Masses with children, young people, the sick, or persons with disabilities, and ritual Masses (for example, funeral or wedding Masses) at which a significant number of the assembly may be non-communicants or non-believers will necessarily impose different demands appropriate to the needs of the occasion.

Choice of Mass and Texts
Chapter VII of *GIRM* invites 'harmonious planning' of the various rites of the Mass so that the most suitable options available are chosen, in conjunction with all those involved in a celebration, so as to help 'dispose the hearts and minds of the faithful to participate in the Eucharist.'[7]

It is worthwhile becoming familiar with the directives offered for the selection of prayers and scripture readings. Certain days (such as Sundays, solemnities and feasts), because of their importance, require that the readings and prayers given in the various books be used. This also gives important expression to the reality of the Church as a communion of communities which, on these occasions, reads the same scriptures and prays the same prayers as its sisters and brothers in other Local Churches throughout the world. The local assembly is able to interpret its own life and happenings in the context of the scriptures proclaimed, in the homily, as well as in the Intercessions. Other occasions allow greater freedom with regard to choice of readings,[8] prayers,[9] and music.[10]

---

[4] *SC* 40
[5] see *GIRM* 113, 115, 116
[6] see *GIRM* 352
[7] *GIRM* 352
[8] *GIRM* 356-362
[9] *GIRM* 363-365
[10] *GIRM* 366-367

CELEBRATING THE MYSTERY OF FAITH

When considering which Eucharistic Prayer is most suitable,[11] attention should be drawn also to the two Eucharistic Prayers for Reconciliation, as well as the Eucharistic Prayer for use in Masses for Various Needs and Occasions. It should be remembered that these Eucharistic Prayers, along with Eucharistic Prayer IV, have *invariable prefaces* and therefore, to preserve their literary integrity, should be employed only when the Mass has no preface of its own (with the exception that a preface on a penitential theme may be used for the Eucharistic Prayers for Reconciliation).

Masses for Various Circumstances

Chapter VIII of *GIRM* outlines the choices available in relation to Masses for Various Needs, Various Circumstances, and Votive Masses[12] and Masses for the Dead.[13] It is worthwhile becoming familiar with the various options proposed here as, in practice, the choices available are not often fully used in pastoral situations.

The final paragraph of this chapter offers a pastoral caution which should inform how choices and adaptations are made in the local assembly and parish. While it is given with specific reference to Funeral Masses, it can be recommended as a guide for the celebration of Christian Marriage as well as other parish and special liturgies: 'Pastors should, moreover, take into special account those who are present at a liturgical celebration or who hear the Gospel on the occasion of the funeral and who may be non-Catholics or Catholics who never or rarely participate in the Eucharist or who seem even to have lost the faith. For priests are ministers of Christ's Gospel for all.'[14]

3. ADAPTATIONS MADE BY BISHOPS AND THE CONFERENCE OF BISHOPS

The first part of Chapter IX looks at changes and adaptations that are made by the local bishop[15] and by the Conference of Bishops.[16] The procedure for making more radical changes is set out in the second part.[17]

The Local Bishop

The short list of practical decisions listed which pertain to the diocesan bishop and the local church community all form part of the important work of the bishop to promote liturgy within his diocese because with him 'lies responsibility above all for fostering the spirit' of the liturgy among his flock.[18]

These decisions include norms on concelebration, the duties of servers, the distribution of Holy Communion under both kinds and the construction and reordering of churches.

The Conference of Bishops

The Conference of Bishops has a responsibility to ensure that:
1. The relevant liturgical books are translated into a language that can 'be proclaimed or sung during an actual celebration.'[19]

---

[11] *GIRM* 364-365
[12] *GIRM* 368-378
[13] *GIRM* 379-385
[14] *GIRM* 385
[15] *GIRM* 387
[16] *GIRM* 389-394
[17] *GIRM* 395-399
[18] see *GIRM* 387, *SC* 41
[19] *GIRM* 389, 391, 392

2. Appropriate music is promoted so as to enable a deeper musical participation of the assembly in the liturgy.[20]
3. Each diocese have its own local calendar and prayers proper to these celebrations – the same should exist for the entire country so that those days which are of particular national or local importance can be suitably celebrated.[21]
4. It is also appropriate that certain texts, as well as gestures and postures, be used at national level.[22] While diverse customs in some matters exist in various parts of the world, there is no reason why a huge variation would exist in these matters between different parishes or dioceses, so it is simply a matter of common sense that adaptations be agreed at Conference level.

A More Thoroughgoing Adaptation

The last part of Chapter IX addresses what it calls 'more thoroughgoing adaptations' that the 'spiritual welfare' people may require, having in mind the younger churches.[23] These final paragraphs[24] set out a procedure where a Local Church initiates adaptations to the liturgy because of its own particular customs and culture. Given the changing nature of our society and the ever increasing cultural complexity that is ours, thanks to the presence among us of peoples from all parts of the world, suggests otherwise. The active involvement of peoples from various Asian, African, Latin American and European cultural backgrounds, and their participation in Church life, will require of us adaptations so as to help them feel part of our common worship. And in a similar way, their welcome presence in our midst modifies our behavioural patterns as well as cultural parameters, and this will require that some changes and adaptations be made *for our sakes* as well.

---

[20] *GIRM 393*
[21] *GIRM 394*
[22] *GIRM 390*
[23] *GIRM 395*, see *SC 37-40*
[24] *GIRM 395-399*

PARISH BASED INTRODUCTION TO *GIRM*

A five-session study on the celebration of Sunday Mass. This is a suitable introduction to GIRM *for a parish liturgy group.*

INTRODUCTION

The publication of the *General Instruction of the Roman Missal* is an ideal moment for the members of any parish community to take time and reflect on the celebration of its liturgy. Many parishes find that they are becoming increasingly confident in preparing and celebrating major events in the liturgical year, but where they need to work a little more is in the preparation and celebration of the Sunday eucharist. This study guide is designed to assist those responsible for liturgy in parish communities in their task.

AIM OF THE SESSIONS

Each session is self-contained but they do flow one from another and it is best to start with session one and work to session five. However, a particular session may be useful in focussing with a particular ministry group, for example, using the session on the Word with readers, cantors and others involved in the Liturgy of the Word in the parish.

STRUCTURE OF THE SESSIONS

The material is laid out in five sessions, which follow the unfolding of the Sunday Eucharist. Each session focuses on the meaning of that section of the Sunday celebration and offers a checklist of practical suggestions that a parish may or may not wish to adapt. What is important is that they lead to discussion among the group and help group members to deepen their knowledge and appreciation for the Sunday Eucharist. The checklist does not make sense without the background offered in the session material itself.

GOING FURTHER

While it is not necessary for everyone in the group to have a copy of the *General Instruction*, it is an aim of this material to give people enough confidence to take up the *General Instruction* or any liturgical book and to begin to work with it. Until the treasures of the liturgical books are unearthed by parish liturgy teams the work of liturgical renewal is only half started.

METHOD

The material can be used in the way that is best for the group. A useful way might be to hold a five night course for the parish liturgy group and use one session per evening. Decide how long the session is going to last and stick with that decision. An hour and a half is often seen as ideal for a group. Perhaps you might want to have tea and coffee at the end of the evening. Make sure that the room you are using is comfortable and allows the group to interact with each other. A candle set in the centre of the room and some soft music can help set a mood of reflection which is key for this kind of work. It is good to begin a session with some prayer perhaps with a passage of scripture and some pointers for personal reflection. Carefully time the length of prayer and pace it well. It is important that each session has a leader, whether that rotates from each week or not. The material can be distributed to the participants the week before the group meets.

Following the prayer the material for that session can be presented to the group or if participants have had time to read it feedback can be taken. Use the material to reflect on the actual practice of your parish. This is not designed to criticise parish practices, but to acknowledge and value what is good in our parish liturgy, what do we need to work on and what could we devote our energies to right now. Not everything can be done at once, so draw up some priorities for your parish. 'The Things to Do' section might be useful in focussing your reflection here.

Key to deepening our experience of liturgy is becoming evermore attentive to the mystery we celebrate. Ultimately liturgy is the work of God in Jesus Christ, it is God's good gift to us freely given and graciously bestowed. We can do our best to prepare the ground of this encounter, but remember it is our response to the saving mystery already given to us in abundance.

EVALUATION

Sometimes evaluation is seen as a bad word, it has suggestions that are negative for some people and for others it is a chance to speak negatively of others. That is not what is suggested here, rather see it as

- an opportunity to value what the parish community and its liturgy team is doing well and
- a moment to explore or note what still awaits your attention!

The purpose of this evaluation is to reflect on what the group has learnt, to explore how that might be brought forward and if this course is to take place again, what might be improved, what might receive more time, what should be emphasised even more strongly.

Depending on the size and the nature of the group using these sessions, an evaluation at the end of each evening may be useful or just one at the end of the course of sessions may be all that is needed. Clarity is needed so that the evaluation suggested here is of the course itself, not the parish liturgy as that is the focus of each of the sessions.

Evaluation should focus on the **physical space** where the course was held. Was it adequate, well heated and ventilated? On the **layout of the evening**, was there sufficient time for input, sharing, group work, prayer? Was the session well focussed or not? What were the learnings for each individual and for the group as a whole? What suggestions might the group have for the next time, in terms of organisation, material for input, structure of the evening?

Evaluation questions are best phrased 'What was helpful...' and 'What was not helpful...'

SESSION 1:
GATHERING – CALLED TO BE THE PEOPLE OF GOD

Any human celebration begins with us coming together: we then speak with each other, share with each other and then take our leave when the celebration comes to an end. Our Eucharistic celebration also follows these four basic elements of human celebration. This evening we are going to spend some time thinking about the first of these movements, the movement of gathering.

GOD'S PEOPLE GATHERED

Every one of us who comes on Sunday morning or evening, is called to take a full, active, prayerful and conscious part in our liturgical celebration. This is our right and our duty as baptised members of the people of God. Some of us serve this assembly as readers, collectors, priest, ministers of holy communion or ministers of song. But each and every one of us shares the ministry of the Eucharist. We are all members of the assembly and form part of the Body of Christ: Christ who offers a prayer of thanksgiving and praise to Father, Christ who offers himself to the Father in this celebration.

We Catholics have always rightly recognised the presence of Christ in the form of bread and wine in our Eucharistic celebrations. Over the last number of years we have grown in our understanding of Christ's presence in his Word, when the Scriptures are proclaimed in the worshipping assembly. The faithful have also recognised the presence of Christ in the priest, who presides over the assembly. But we have often overlooked or not even recognised that the first and fundamental presence of Christ is the assembly itself, those who have gathered together to celebrate the liturgy. We have, in short, forgotten about the immense dignity that each one of us has received in the holy sacrament of baptism: I don't expect the person sitting next to me to be a sign of Christ's presence for me and I certainly don't expect myself to be a means of Christ's presence to those who gather around me and beyond into my daily life!

GATHERING AND INTRODUCTORY RITES

The very first thing any group does when it comes together is to say why they gather! So too when the Christian community comes to celebrate the Eucharist, the community gathers and says who they are. We are God's holy people, the Body of Christ, coming together as a community to listen to God's word and celebrate the Eucharist together. The community is named as the Body of Christ. This is a little different from past practices when looking around in Church or even glancing to see who was sitting beside or behind was positively discouraged. Perhaps we could look around as we begin our celebration, be aware of the presence of other people: Who is here as we gather to celebrate? What stories of joy and stories of sorrow are they bringing with them into this celebration?

This section of the Mass is made up of the entrance song, the greeting, penitential rite, *Kyrie*, *Gloria*, and opening prayer. The entrance song accompanies the procession and introduces the mystery of the season or feast that we are celebrating. After the kissing of the altar and when the singing has ended, priest and people make the sign of the cross. This greeting reminds all of us present that we stand in the presence of the Lord. We manifest and make present the Church in this place. The penitential rite or the blessing and sprinkling of water that follows reminds us to celebrate worthily these holy mysteries. The *Kyrie (Lord, have mercy)* praises the Lord and implores his mercy. God's glory is praised in the *Gloria*. After the priest invites us to pray, we spend some time in silence realising that we are in God's presence and we make our prayer, the prayer that we are carrying in our hearts for the week that is beginning, the worries and the joys that we wish to be transformed in this Eucharist. This prayer is gathered up by the priest and the assembly responds with the acclamation: *Amen*. In their directions for posture at Mass, the Irish Bishops note that we should stand for this part of the Eucharist. Standing is the posture of the Christian called to the immense dignity of the baptised, standing is the external sign that we are ready to enter into communion with our God.

THINGS TO DO

- How do you and your liturgy group see the assembly? Are you convinced that the assembly of believers is a most important and powerful symbol of the liturgy? Have a discussion about posture both for these rites and for the whole Eucharistic celebration. Perhaps you may need to engage in a catechesis with the assembly.

- Why not invite the presider and the ministers to be at the door of the church to greet and welcome the people as they come into the church this morning. This is the time for words of welcome, not during the Introduction, which is about something else. Have the presider and the ministers process through the body of the Church; if you have a deacon, have him carry the *Book of the Gospels* in the procession or in the absence of a deacon have a minister of the Word carry it. The song that accompanies the procession is to open the celebration and set the tone of the season or the feast that we are celebrating; make sure it is something that everyone can sing.

- Decide to use the sprinkling rite today. Use a large jug and bowl and have the water poured after the prayer of blessing, move through the assembly and really sprinkle the people. Have the assembly or the choir sing a suitable song to accompany the sprinkling.

- Think about how your community might extend or even initiate a ministry of welcome to your parish celebrations. Who do you welcome this morning? How many new people in the assembly have you greeted and welcomed? Is the Church warm and bright enough to encourage people to participate? Make sure that the altar and the worship space are free of clutter and are well decorated. Have the candles lit well before people gather.

- The *Kyrie (Lord, have mercy)* is a litany which praises the Lord and implores his mercy; it is not about the assembly protesting its sinfulness.

- The gathering rites conclude with the Collect or Opening Prayer. Allow a good space of time between the invitation 'Let us pray' and the rest of the prayer. Give the assembly time to pray in the silence of their hearts, so that the Collect might truly be a collection of the prayers of the Body of Christ. This is something that you can build up to over a number of weeks and you may need to even underline it in the invitation to prayer: 'Let us pray in silence […]'.

- Don't overdo it! The purpose of the gathering rites is to gather, to name and to prepare the assembly to listen to the Word of God. Some assemblies arrive at that point exhausted because all that has gone before the Word of God.

SESSION 2:
THE LITURGY OF THE WORD – LISTENING AND RESPONDING

After we have prayed and prepared ourselves, the assembly now sits to listen to God's word proclaimed in the scriptures. The Liturgy of the Word is made up of readings from scripture and chants between the readings; these are developed and completed in the Homily, Profession of Faith and the Prayer of the Faithful. The readings are for us today the Word of God. God's word proclaimed and listened to is the foundation of all that the Church does:

> When the scriptures are read in the Church, God himself speaks to his people, and it is Christ, present in his word, who proclaims the Gospel. (*GIRM* 29)

CHRIST AMONG US AS WORD – LISTENING

The function of the Liturgy of the Word is to celebrate the mystery of Christ's presence among us. When we listen to the Word of God proclaimed to us, we are been fed. Just as the assembly is fed from the table of the Lord in the Eucharist, so too we are fed from the table of God's Word. This Word is a Word for our lives and about our lives as Christians. In reflecting on this Word, on allowing it to become part of our experience, the word mingles with our lives. This calls for listening on all our parts, that hearing which is called for when something really important is being communicated. The American Bishops have expressed this kind of listening well:

> Listening is not an isolated moment. It is a way of life. It means openness to the Lord's voice not only in the Scriptures but in the events of our daily lives and in the experience of our brothers and sisters. It is not just listening but our listening together for the Lord's word to the community. (*Fulfilled in your Hearing*, 20)

The text that has been read to us is not about handing on something that comes from the past, rather it is pointing to what God is doing here and now. Proclamation of the word of God tells the assembly how God is acting among them. We listen to this fact in the Word of God, we sing in the words of the Responsorial Psalm. The Gospel reading is the highlight of the Liturgy of the Word – the other readings point toward it, all that follows flows from it. We know something important is happening when we see the book carried and kissed, surrounded with candles and reverenced with incense. Christ is present and speaking to his people. The Homily, which follows the Gospel reading, is again a proclamation of the good news of what God has done for a beloved people. Silence follows the Homily. Our proclamation of the Creed is the profession of faith that we share with Christians all over the world. The Prayer of the Faithful concludes the Liturgy of the Word. These invitations to prayer are an expression of our care and concern for the world in which we live and for which we have committed ourselves to pray. These prayers are an expression of the priestly function of all believers. The intentions that we pray for are for local and universal concerns: while we pray for the sick of the parish, we must include all those who are sick, that they may know the healing power of Christ. As a gathered assembly we exercise our responsibility and our task as the holy people of God to intercede for all as Christ, the Beloved One of God, gave his life for all.

We sit to listen to the Lord who is our one true teacher. We stand in the presence of the Gospel, as we give our assent to these words of life. We sit for the Homily, as the presider applies these saving words to our life as a community and we stand once more to proclaim our faith a and pray for all creation in the Prayer of the Faithful.

THINGS TO DO

- Allow a period of silence after the first and the second readings; silence can also follow the homily. People will get used to it and it can be built on over a period of time. Teach the assembly to allow the readings echo in their hearts: are they struck by a word or a phrase? Allow that to enter their hearts and become their prayer. Encourage the assembly to allow the refrain from the Responsorial Psalm become their prayer for the week. With the practice of silence the assembly will become a place of stillness despite babies fussing and people coughing! Silence is not just the absence of noise, it is the entering of a still place where we can truly hear and respond to the Word we have heard proclaimed. Silence is an essential aspect of all liturgy, it allows for balance and rhythm in our celebration.

- The Responsorial Psalm can often be the key to understanding the liturgy of a given Sunday. Pay attention to it and allow it to form your preparation. If at all possible it should be sung, or perhaps your parish community could decide to learn ten or twelve psalms each year.

- Have a Gospel procession during the singing of the *Alleluia*. It needs the sweet smell of incense, the carrying of candles and the processing of the book to let us know that we are indeed going to hear good news.

- Could a cantor sing the intentions of the Prayer of the Faithful? The texts should be short and direct. Add one or two new intercessions each week; they can be inspired by the readings of this Sunday and by the events of the past week. Use the same response for the assembly each week and it is amazing how quickly it becomes part of their heritage. Begin by singing the response.

- Encourage the assembly to prepare the readings during the week. Maybe put next Sunday's scripture references in the parish bulletin. Encourage the assembly to use the refrain from the responsorial psalm as their constant prayer during the coming week.

- If your parish has a family Mass, have you thought about bringing the children out for a Children's Liturgy of the Word and if you do have it, make sure it is connected to the assembly's prayer.

SESSION 3:
THE LITURGY OF THE EUCHARIST – LET US GIVE THANKS AND PRAISE

We are often told that part of Irish tradition is to count one's blessings. It is part of that understanding of the world that sees everything given to us as gift. So too is the Eucharist: it is the remembering of the greatest of God's gifts, the gift of Jesus.

PREPARING THE GIFTS

The Liturgy of the Eucharist begins with the presentation of the gifts – members of the assembly bring forward the bread and wine, symbols of all that we have and are and which will be transformed for us into the body and blood of Christ. Offerings of money or gifts for the poor can also be brought forward at this moment. As the priest prepares the gifts and the altar, we prepare ourselves for the great Eucharistic Prayer, a prayer of thanksgiving and praise for all the wonders that God has done for each of us and the supreme gift of God, the gift of Jesus the Beloved One of God.

GIVING THANKS

We have come to the core and the centre of Sunday Eucharist. These words that become so familiar to us week after week can become so part of our minds that we often forget what they mean and what they invite us to. Our Eucharistic Prayers remind us of Jewish heritage and they are closely related to various forms of Jewish prayers. These prayers bless God for all that God has done for us and thank God for all the good gifts of the earth. We recall in these prayers the wonderful deeds that God has done in the past and we implore God to do these deeds again in our day. This type of prayer would have been familiar to Jesus and his disciples and would have formed the main part of the prayer at the Last Supper, just as it was part of the prayer at all Jewish meals. Early Christians continued to pray in this way when they gathered to celebrate the Eucharist and to fulfil the command of Jesus 'to do this in memory of him'. Our Eucharistic Prayers reflect this fundamental understanding of prayer. We begin every prayer with the invitation: 'Let us give God thanks and praise.' We remember the wonders of creation and the covenant, the preaching of the prophets and the lives of the prophets. The prayer then recalls the death and the resurrection of Jesus, the very foundation of our faith. We ask God to continue to protect us and grant us help. As the prayer continues the priest prays that we be gathered into unity as God's holy Church. We pray for the leaders of the Church and for the living and the dead, and that one day we all share the life of the saints, all the holy ones that have gone before us. The prayer always ends with the great doxology leading into the Great Amen. As an assembly we have three great acclamations in the prayer: the Holy, Holy, when we join our praise with the opening praise of God in the preface; the memorial acclamation when we acclaim the greatest of God's saving action, the death and resurrection of Christ and the Great Amen when we affirm with our lips and our hearts the whole sweep of the prayer.

THE MODEL OF ALL OUR PRAYING

One of the great challenges facing us is to make the Eucharistic Prayer part of our daily life. We can easily make the prayer of blessing part of our day. When we get up in the mornings 'Blessed are you, Lord our God, for the gift of another day of life'; before and after our meals we can thank God for the gift of food and family life 'We thank you, God of the living, for all that is good…' and add one or two reasons for each day, including the gift of food placed before us. The same with after meals. It does help our appreciation of the Eucharistic Prayer and brings its spirit into everyday. The posture established by the Bishops in their norms is kneeling or in special circumstances, standing. Both are postures of prayer, respect and wonder at the goodness of God.

THINGS TO DO

- Have the procession of the gifts – it should move through the assembly: so the gifts need to be placed among them. Don't overdo it. This part of the liturgy is a time of preparation within the entire sweep of the Liturgy of the Eucharist. As such, it is a minor element.

- There is no need for music every Sunday at the preparation of the gifts: sometimes allow silence, as the altar is prepared. The altar should be bare till this point or just covered with a cloth. On it are placed the paten of bread, the chalice and the book. The altar is not the place for floral decorations: the gifts of God should be clearly seen by all and not blocked by candles, bookstands or microphones. If the gifts of money are received at this point, they should be placed near the altar and not on it. This collection should take place before the presentation of the bread and wine.

- If there is no singing at this point, the presider may pray the given prayers. If there is music, the prayers are to be prayed inaudibly, that means in silence and there is no need to mouth the words.

- For presiders: Be sure to remember that it is the whole assembly who prays the Eucharistic Prayer. The priest prays it in the name of Christ, the head of his body, his beloved church. Gather the assembly in with your prayer and your gesture, be warm and generous in your gesture. This prayer has to be prayed from the heart, with strong faith and over time should be memorised. Sing the preface. Use the gestures indicated for the great Eucharistic Prayer. Work towards singing most of the prayer and teaching the assembly the responses. Vary the prayer that you use: in Family Masses do you use the Eucharistic Prayers for Masses with Children? Maybe now is the time to start and teach the children and the adults the responses.

- Encourage the assembly to pray before and after meals each day. It provides a powerful link with the great prayer of thanksgiving that is the Eucharistic Prayer. From time to time give examples in the parish bulletin, vary them according to the liturgical season.

SESSION 4:
SENT TO SERVE

At the end of the Eucharistic Prayer we acclaim our *Amen* – so be it, just as you have said. We are agreeing in the depths of our heart and with our voice with all that God has done for us in the past and what God continues to do for us right now.

COMING TO COMMUNION

We now stand for the Lord's Prayer, the great prayer of all the baptised. Before we come forward to share the holy gifts of the Lord's table we have to make sure that we are at peace with each other and with the world. The Lord's Prayer, in its request for daily bread, brings naturally to mind the Eucharist. In its call to forgiveness, we pledge to forgive others just as God has forgiven us. This leads naturally into the sharing of the sign of peace. A ritual of sharing peace is as old as the New Testament and one that has been part of the Eucharist since the early centuries of the Church. It is not a ritual of welcoming, or even one of hospitality: it is a prayer that Christ's peace truly fill our lives and the lives of those with whom we are about to share the Lord's Body and Blood. This recalls the reminder that Paul gave to the Church in Corinth: if we eat and drink the Body and the Blood of the Lord, without seeing the Body of Christ in his disciples, we eat and drink a judgement on ourselves.

THE BREAKING OF BREAD

One of the earliest, if not the earliest description of the celebration of the Eucharist, we find in the Acts of the Apostles. There the Eucharist is described as the breaking of bread: 'They devoted themselves to the apostles' instruction and the communal life, to the breaking of bread and the prayers' (Acts 2:42). This gesture is one that is highly symbolic: just as the bread is broken into many parts, so too we who share it become one body in Christ. Coming to communion is the high point and the culmination of the Eucharistic celebration; it is the goal of the whole sweep of the celebration. It can be understood in so many ways and has been over the centuries of the history of the Church. It has been seen as the sealing of a new covenant with God this time in the Blood of Christ: as passing with Christ through death and now sharing his resurrection: as a foretaste of the Kingdom of God where there will be enough to eat and drink-bread of life and cup of joy for a world that is filled with brokenness and sorrow; sharing in the communion that is the very life of God. As we stand and receive communion in the midst of the assembly, we enter into once more the covenant that is offered to each one of us. We say *Amen* to being the Body of Christ in the world; we say *Amen* to give our lives in Christ for the life of the world. It is an awesome moment indeed.

Our posture for this part of the Eucharistic is standing and processing. As a risen people we stand in respect for the Lord who comes to meet us.

THINGS TO DO
- Encourage the assembly to stand at the beginning of the Lord's Prayer by occasionally inviting them: 'Let us stand and pray the great prayer of Jesus' or 'Let us stand and pray for the coming of God's Kingdom'.
- Even though the sign of peace has been restored for nearly thirty years now, it is no harm to remind parishioners of it and its meaning. It can be part of a homily dealing with the Eucharist or an insert in the parish bulletin and part of sacramental preparation evenings and courses.
- Nowhere in the Church's liturgy or in the rubrics of *Roman Missal* is the practice of distributing hosts consecrated at another Mass described. It certainly does not show a right understanding of the Eucharistic Prayer and the gathered assembly. Taking hosts from the

tabernacle is something that should happen only rarely when something has happened that has led to too few consecrated hosts at this liturgy. Bread and wine consecrated during the Mass is to be for us communion in the Body and Blood of the Lord at the same Mass.

- Have the cantor lead the litany 'Lamb of God' and allow it to continue till all the consecrated and blessed bread is broken and ready for communion.

- The breaking of bread also meant the very practical breaking of bread before the introduction of small hosts. It was this action that was accompanied by the singing of 'Lamb of God.' The text explains the action: Christ's body and blood are broken and poured for our sakes. If this action takes longer than the usual three invocations, they may be repeated or new ones added to lengthen the litany: 'Bread of Life, you take away the sins of the world, have mercy on us.' As a parish community this needs reflection – the current practice of just breaking the priest's host is not a reflection of the one bread that we are called to share. A useful reference to begin this reflection is the *General Instruction of the Roman Missal* 321.

SESSION 5:
MAKING LINKS WITH LITURGY AND LIFE

The noted Italian Servite priest and poet, David Maria Turoldo, regularly dismissed the Sunday assembly with the words: 'The Eucharist never ends, but let us go in peace.' While we might question the liturgical propriety of the dismissal, the underlying idea is clear and the link with the rest of the week clearly established. Linking what we as a Christian community celebrate in the Eucharist and how we live the rest of the week is at times obscure and very often just forgotten about. The duty is done and put away until next Sunday is a common enough reaction even among very committed Christians. But the concluding rites of the Sunday Eucharist tell the Sunday assembly clearly: 'Go in peace to love and serve the Lord.' Where else do we love and serve the Lord but in the people with whom we share our lives, those who live around us and those with whom we share this earth!

For Christians the mystery of God celebrated in the liturgy and the mystery of community, those gathered around the word and the table cannot be separated. For the Eucharist is lived out, deepened and shared in the rest of the week. In our Sunday Eucharist we come face to face with God's desire for the world, the way the world should be, how the reign of God would take hold of our earth. A world of plenty is promised in our Eucharist, where all would have enough to eat and drink; a world of justice is promised in our Eucharist, where the division between strangers is broken down and we call each other brother and sister.

TO BE WHAT WE CELEBRATE
To live the Christian vision with fidelity and love is hard and it challenges much of what passes as normal around us. Striving to be Christian is about becoming Church, being the people of God and which is what we are in a unique way when we gather for worship. But we are not Church for ourselves. Being truly Church, engaging in liturgy in a deep way calls us, dares us to be this way in the rest of life, not just as individuals but as a community: to be human, to be community, to be the people of God. At the end of the day, true prayer for the world throws us right back into the world and longing for its transformation.

For our liturgy to even to begin to challenge us to these realities, it must be strongly celebrated with respect for symbol and ritual. What is not being called for is any attempt for the liturgy to become a consciousness raising exercise. Liturgy is worship of God and any other use of liturgy is manipulation. But in worshipping God, we are challenged in a way that no other exercise would challenge us: we are called to be what we celebrate. To be the Body of Christ in the world, to see each other as the Body of Christ, to recognise in the breaking of the bread the body of Christ is a constant learning, but it is one that we are called to each Sunday and one that we are sent out to live in the rest of the week as we seek to be the Body of Christ for a broken and glorious world.

THINGS TO DO
* Establish links between the liturgy group and groups in the parish and the local community who are involved in the struggle for justice at home and abroad.
* See that liturgical celebrations in your community regularly pray for justice and are linked with ongoing campaigns in the Church e.g. the Trocaire Lenten Campaign. These can form part of the intentions of the Prayer of the Faithful.

- In terms of relationship to the parish and its structures it is vital that these lines are clear to the member of the liturgy group and other groups in the parish community. What is the task of the liturgy group needs to be carefully defined when a group is established. What are the lines of communication to the Parish Pastoral Council needs to be carefully tended.
- In what ways does our parish community exist beyond our Sunday Eucharist? How might we extend its fellowship beyond our worship, that it might become 'the liturgy after the liturgy'?